Choosing
Books for Children

The Sea Egg by L M Boston, illustrated by Peter Boston

Choosing
Books for Children

Peter Hollindale

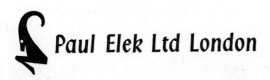

Paul Elek Ltd London

For Anne

ISBN 0 236 15492 6

© Peter Hollindale 1974

First published in 1974 by
Paul Elek Ltd
54–58 Caledonian Road
London N1 9RN
Reprinted and revised 1975

Printed in Great Britain by
A. Wheaton & Company, Exeter

Author's acknowledgements

I am grateful to the many children, parents and teachers who have contributed their ideas to this book, and particularly to Miss Mollie Haigh and pupils at Easingwold School, and Smestow School, Wolverhampton. Her preparation of the index is only part of my wife's unfailing practical help and encouragement; I have dedicated to her a book which is already in large measure her own.

The publisher and I are also grateful for permission to reproduce illustrations from :

L M Boston, *The Sea Egg*, illustrated by Peter Boston (Faber); Maurice Sendak, *Where the Wild Things Are* (Bodley Head); Pat Hutchins, *Rosie's Walk* (Bodley Head); Ivor Cutler, *Meal One*, illustrated by Helen Oxenbury (Heinemann); 'BB', *The Little Grey Men*, illustrated by Denys Watkins-Pitchford (Methuen); Mollie Hunter, *Thomas and the Warlock*, illustrated by Charles Keeping (Blackie); Henri Bosco, *The Boy and the River*, illustrated by Lynton Lamb (Oxford University Press); Joan Aiken, *The Wolves of Willoughby Chase*, illustrated by Pat Marriott (Cape); Lewis Carroll, *Alice Through the Looking-Glass*, illustrated by John Tenniel (Macmillan); K M Peyton, *Flambards*, illustrated by Victor Ambrus (Oxford University Press); P H Newby, *The Spirit of Jem*, illustrated by Keith Vaughan (Kestrel); Leon Garfield, *Jack Holborn*, illustrated by Antony Maitland (Kestrel).

and to include extracts from :

Graham Greene, 'The Lost Childhood', *Collected Essays* (Bodley Head); *The Use of English*, Vol. XVIII, Winter 1966; Helen Morgan, *Mrs Pinny and the Blowing Day* (Faber); Ruth Tomalin, *The Sea Mice: An Adventure* (Faber); Alison Uttley,

Secret Places and Other Essays (Faber); C S Lewis, *The Last Battle* (Bodley Head); Diana Trilling, 'Tom Sawyer – Delinquent', introduction to Mark Twain, *The Adventures of Tom Sawyer* (© The Crowell-Collier Publishing Co., 1962); Cynthia Harnett, *The Writing on the Hearth* (Methuen); Leon Garfield, *The Drummer Boy* (Kestrel); Michael Innes, *The Journeying Boy* (Gollancz and Mr J I M Stewart); K M Peyton, *Flambards* (Oxford University Press); George Orwell, 'Boys' Weeklies', *Collected Essays* (Secker & Warburg and Mrs Sonia Brownell Orwell).

Contents

PART ONE

1 The Problems of Choosing 13
2 Consumer Reactions 30

PART TWO

Note on Using the Book-Lists 37
3 The Pre-school Child: Flowers in the Carpet 40
Book-List for the Pre-school Child 53
4 The First Years at School: Neighbours and Strangers 58
Book-List for the First Years at School 70
5 From Junior School to Secondary: The Immediate
World 76
Book-List for Junior School to Secondary (1) 90
6 From Junior School to Secondary: Wider Horizons 94
Book-List for Junior School to Secondary (2) 110
7 What Place for the Classics? 115
Book-List of the Classics 128
8 Adolescent Reading 135
Book-List for Adolescent Reading 146

PART THREE

9 A Contrast of Problems: Enid Blyton and
William Mayne 153
10 The World of the Comic: 'Aaargh!' 159
11 Television and Competing Media 168
12 Slow, Backward or Reluctant? 175
13 Further Information 179
Index 183

List of Illustrations

The Sea Egg by L M Boston, illustrated by Peter Boston
(Faber)   *Frontis.*
Where the Wild Things Are by Maurice Sendak (Bodley
Head)   44
Rosie's Walk by Pat Hutchins (Bodley Head)   47
Meal One by Ivor Cutler, illustrated by Helen Oxenbury
(Heinemann)   52
The Little Grey Men by 'BB', illustrated by Denys
Watkins-Pitchford (Methuen)   62
Thomas and the Warlock by Mollie Hunter, illustrated
by Charles Keeping (Blackie)   69
The Boy and the River by Henri Bosco, illustrated by
Lynton Lamb (Oxford)   85
The Wolves of Willoughby Chase by Joan Aiken, illus-
trated by Pat Marriott (Cape)   106
Alice Through the Looking-Glass by Lewis Carroll,
illustrated by John Tenniel   123
Flambards by K M Peyton, illustrated by Victor Ambrus
(Oxford)   138
The Spirit of Jem by P H Newby, illustrated by Keith
Vaughan (Kestrel)   145
Jack Holborn by Leon Garfield, illustrated by Antony
Maitland (Kestrel)   165

List of Illustrations

Part One

1 The Problems of Choosing

'Perhaps it is only in childhood that books have any deep influence on our lives. In later life we admire, we are entertained, we may modify some views we already hold, but we are more likely to find in books merely a confirmation of what is in our minds already: as in a love affair it is our own features that we see reflected flatteringly back.

But in childhood all books are books of divination, telling us about the future, and like the fortune teller who sees a long journey in the cards or death by water, they influence the future. I suppose that is why books excited us so much. What do we ever get nowadays from reading to equal the excitement and revelation in those first fourteen years? Of course I should be interested to hear that a new novel by Mr E M Forster was going to appear this spring, but I could never compare that mild expectation of civilised pleasure with the missed heartbeat, the appalled glee I felt when I found on a library shelf a novel by Rider Haggard, Percy Westerman, Captain Brereton or Stanley Weyman which I had not read before. No, it is in those early years that I would look for the crisis, the moment when life took a new slant in its journey towards death.'

(Graham Greene, 'The Lost Childhood')

A child's shiver of excited discovery is the experience that prompts this book—the sense of a world opening, a new raid on the unknown and the unexplained. For a child destined to become a distinguished novelist, like Graham Greene, it is hardly a surprising experience, and his testimony resembles those of many other writers. From novelists' autobiographies one forms a strong impression that the best form of upbringing is to be let loose in a large library (often one's father's, and containing some highly unsuitable scriptures), and to divide one's time between unsupervised reading and unsupervised exploration of the countryside, formal education being pared to the minimum.

But this early excited discovery of books is not the sole prerogative of those who will later write them. You can see it in any children's library on any Saturday morning. And Greene is surely right about its transience, too : if you walk through into the adult library, you will not find it there. Certainly you will find pleasures anticipated, but the tremble, the nerve-end joy will have gone.

For some children it will never come, no matter what efforts are made by sympathetic adults. But for most, it can, and the fault is in ourselves, as parents and teachers, if it fails to shine at all or is prematurely snuffed out. It may be inevitable that with the passage of time it will subside to the modest glow of adult enjoyment that Greene describes, a glow which warms a little, and brightens a little, rather than a blaze which burns and illuminates. But without the early childhood enthusiasm it is unlikely that the later, lifelong glow will come.

Like Greene, I do not value these early excitements just for their intensity of pleasure—though I do value that for its own sake—nor for their power to forge the cooler if more durable satisfactions of later life—though I think they have such a power. Like him, I see them as experiences which may be critical in shaping a personality and affecting the bent of a lifetime.

'BB' (Denys Watkins-Pitchford) has written his best-known children's books for very young children; *The Little Grey Men* won the Carnegie Medal, and has been followed by a host of delightful books, such as *The Forest of Boland Light Railway*. My own debt to 'BB', however, is chiefly for a book for older children, *Brendon Chase*. This is the first book that I can now recall which stirred and excited me, and revealed to me a sense of possibilities in life that I knew to be significant, as Rider Haggard and Co did for Greene. *Brendon Chase* is the story of some boys who, in quarantine for measles, escape from their confinement and run off to fend for themselves in a nearby forest. The story captivated me, and it was enhanced by the deeply atmospheric beauty of the author's illustrations. From forests to islands, from cut-off, self-reliant children to adults in similar, or deeper, or starker predicaments, there is a line of communication between *Brendon Chase* and the works which years later had, and have, a decisive effect on my angle of vision. *Brendon Chase* was followed by *Silver Flame*, a little-known book for children by the late Kenneth Allsop; later came C S Forester's *Brown on Resolution*; later still William Golding's *Lord of the Flies*; and the line leads on to Shakespeare's *Tempest* and *As You Like It* and to Conrad's *Victory* and *Nostromo*. But I can still remember that escape from the Dower House, the charcoal burner's hut, and the dappled glooms of Brendon Chase. Lost in the story to an extent that I could never be nowadays, I was also personally involved in it in ways I did not understand, or need to.

I think these early excitements are important in various ways, which I shall try to explain as we go along. The object of this book is to suggest the value and necessity of these excitements, and to help parents and teachers to provide them. There are two distinct problems here, and we need to keep them separate at the outset, though they will run in harness throughout the book. First, *what* should we provide? Second, *how* should we provide it?

What should we provide?

In the course of the book I shall be proposing some specific answers to this question, thinking of particular age-groups, particular authors, particular topics and types of book. Behind these specific matters there lie some wider questions which we need to look at first. The widest of all is this : even if we accept the need to nourish the child's imagination, why should we use books to do it? These days we have other media readily at hand, especially television and films : won't they do just as well?

They will certainly do a great deal, and in Chapter 11 I shall be looking briefly at their roles, and their relationship with the world of books. Of course they have a role, and a valuable one, which is generally accepted. Not many teachers could now be found making the lofty comprehensive pronouncements about the 'evil effects of the goggle-box', which were customary a few years ago. But their role is additional to books, not instead of them, for the main reason that they provide an experience which is *primarily* pictorial, whereas books supply one which is *primarily* linguistic.

Functionally, a child acquires language as a pre-requisite of acquiring other forms of knowledge and skill. It is the raw material from which he becomes able—with a speed of development which is dramatically evident in the early years—to formulate and organise his thinking; and abundant evidence has been collected during the last few years which demonstrates the crucial connection between early language acquisition and later educational achievement. For the child, language is also by far his most important way of making contact with his fellows, establishing relationships with them, and making judgements about them. Meeting a total stranger face to face, we have visual evidence which helps us to know and be known; on the telephone, we hear a voice which tells us by tone, accent and the like, more than the simple meaning of the words it speaks. But in a letter (or a newspaper, or a legal document) we make contact by words alone. Apart from these basic functions of language, it is also a game of skill, which we practise with daily enjoyment from the beginning—language is no sooner acquired by an infant than it becomes material for play, and he quickly becomes able to appreciate the often elaborate language games of which nursery rhymes are composed.

It is essential that this vigorous language activity which begins in infancy should continue throughout childhood. The 'decline in literacy' is often discussed and often exaggerated, but there is quite enough evidence of low reading standards among older schoolchildren to cause some alarm. Children do not learn to read once and for all, as they learn to tell the time or tie their shoelaces; they acquire an initial skill which then develops throughout childhood, and the extent of its development is deeply influenced by parental assistance and encouragement. Reading is only one kind of language activity among several, but it is not one which can be left to look after itself, or consigned wholly to the teacher.

It is true, of course, that films and television programmes are often excellently scripted, but language can never be their chief concern, because they depend first of all on continuous *pictures*, which have a more immediate, more direct impact than the words which accompany them. There is no substitute for imaginative experience in which language, heard or seen, is given pride of place, and for that we need books. Books to read, books to have read to us.

Does it matter *which* books, though? If we get children to listen to stories, and later to read stories for themselves, should we bother about the quality of what is read? For that matter, how can we know what makes one story for children better than another?

These are much more difficult questions, and they go on causing a good deal of disagreement among teachers, librarians, and others who are professionally concerned with children's reading. There are those who say that the first priority is to establish a reading habit, and if this is done on an unvarying diet of Enid Blyton—well, better that than nothing. Some people would now go further and say that attempts to interest children in 'better' books are thinly disguised campaigns to superimpose established cultural values on defenceless children. In diametric opposition there are others who insist that our job is to introduce children to work which is excellent, and protect them from the second-rate. In this controversy we are up against a recurrent dilemma of modern education : the virtue of 'excellence' often seems incompatible with other virtues, such as breadth, and flexibility, and tolerance. If a librarian tries to exclude Blyton from a library, as one recently did, he is accused of representing a cultural Gestapo. If he allows a free-for-all and tries to meet his customers' demands, he is told that he is lowering standards.

Teachers as well as librarians face this difficulty. In the summer of 1966 Dennis Butts wrote an article in *The Use of English* criticising some of the books chosen by CSE boards for examination work. Amongst others, he described works by

Nicholas Monsarrat and Geoffrey Household as 'rubbish'. The response was prompt, and included a letter from Mr V F Slade which replied as follows:—

'. . . reading is an acquired habit which begins at the level of the reader's age, ability and experience, and . . . these must, initially, dictate selection; . . . whatever illuminates or sharpens or extends the reader's experience is valuable; and (the teacher's) primary concern should not be to give his pupils a taste for what is in the very best taste, but to create a taste for reading, and to encourage discrimination in reading by the example and action of his own intelligence and experience. His aim should not be the "serious study of literature" in the hope that in "contact" with it something will rub off.'

There is some truth on both sides, and we are not faced simply with a problem of selection. Mr Slade stresses the importance of the teacher's role, and it must be widened to include the roles of librarians, and above all parents: our manner of introducing books is just as important as our choice. Few people would reject Mr Butts' ideal that children should be given the chance to read and study great literature, but the weight of experience suggests that we can afford a more relaxed and painless journey towards Parnassus than some writers (not Mr Butts) prescribe. All too frequently, we hear the sound of cultural whips cracking along the route.

The 'weight of experience' is not hidden in volumes of research into children's reading, important and valuable as these are. It lies in the recollected experience of the normal adult reader—the person who reads more than the newspaper. It lies even in the frank admissions of writers who are now concerned to eliminate the dross from contemporary children's reading. It lies, almost certainly, in the memory of anyone reading this book. All of us, surely, read in our childhood a great deal of rubbish; if we are honest, most of us still do. Once we read comics, trivial adventure stories, children's annuals; we did not spurn the adventures of Biggles, and Worrals, or recoil in distaste from sagas of football or ponies. Perhaps our literacy, our ability to enjoy great literature, was permanently crippled by these experiences—but I have not heard anyone confess it. Perhaps things were different then, and nowadays there are more subversive influences from which children need to be protected? This may be so: and from time to time I shall be indicating a few danger spots, of one kind or another. Whether an over-selective reading schedule offers the best form of protection is another matter. This at least is true: I have never been told by anyone that his interest in reading was cut short by Capt W E Johns, but I have often been told that this was the result of premature exposure to detailed study of Shakespeare, or the boredom of an ill-chosen 'form reader'.

There is an elementary mistake which is commonly made, especially by those who readily acknowledge their own past pleasures and in the same breath try to deprive their children of them. The mistake is to draw false comparisons between adult reading habits and children's. As adults we do indeed have habits; our custom is to repeat the same patterns year by year. We read only the racing page; we read nothing but bookstall sexology; we read classics downstairs and whodunnits in the bedroom; we read women's weeklies, or women's monthlies, but probably not both; we read, much or little, good or bad, *regularly*, and we are not to be put off. Children are not like that. They look at books experimentally, and provided that their earliest experiences are not disheartening, they do so with an expectation of pleasure. Where pleasure is not forthcoming, the book is rejected. Where it is plentiful they demand more of the same. Tastes arise and wither unexpectedly; different levels of interest overlap and coincide and jostle for supremacy. Everything is in the melting pot: taste and habit are not settled states but growing, living things, capable of endless mutation and change. Parents and teachers can keep the pot simmering if they know how—aware, perhaps, like Graham Greene, of excitements they can no longer feel themselves. They can also put the fire out and let the pot go cold. They can create a taste for reading, trusting the child to look in fits and starts for something better, or they can dull the taste, usually by choosing the diet, and choosing wrongly.

19

Allowing and encouraging free, experimental reading, much of which will probably be rubbish, does not mean that we have to sacrifice our own sense of what is good, or abdicate all responsibility for choice. It means presenting that choice with reticence, in a form which respects the child's judgement as well as our own, but recognising the occasions when it is essential to intervene.

Obviously the 'enjoyment' principle is an important one, but equally obviously it has its limits. For the adult reader there may be value in a novel which he does not particularly enjoy; for the child reader pleasure and value are not separable in this way. There is a crucial distinction here and failure to grasp it explains the premature exposure to 'classics' which many children undergo, in school if not at home. A young reader is likely to be harmed or discouraged by compulsory attention to a story he does not like.

Unfortunately he may also be harmed by things he *does* enjoy, especially certain books mainly intended for adults, or books which overstep some conventions of the children's book. As an extreme example of this, consider two works of adult non-fiction—Lord Russell of Liverpool's *The Scourge of the Swastika* and *The Knights of Bushido*, widely-known books which describe and illustrate the wartime atrocities of the Germans and the Japanese. The announced purpose of these books is to prevent these crimes from falling into premature oblivion and keep alive a public indignation and watchfulness which will guard against any recurrence of such things. Most praiseworthy, indeed. When these books circulate widely in paperback, however, they fall into the hands of young readers who may not react in the manner required. The boys I taught who had read these books were chiefly interested in the details of near-naked figures being whipped or racked or otherwise tortured and mutilated. Far from being indignant about it all, they were intrigued and stimulated by the sub-human behaviour these exhibited. It is perfectly common for adolescent boys to indulge in fantasies of violence, and for most boys such books provide a harmless if gruesome excitement which will soon give place to more innocent and practical carnalities. For a few, however, they are an experience of sado-masochistic relish which may lastingly inhibit sexual and emotional growth. It is by no means uncommon for propagandist art, in the widest sense (Lord Russell's books are certainly not works of art in anything but the widest sense) to encourage the very appetites it outwardly condemns, and my own experience is that these particular books unquestionably provided for some boys a source of injurious pleasure.

Other books for adults supply seemingly comparable pleasures —the work of Micky Spillane for instance (which is brilliantly satirised in a short story by Evan Hunter entitled 'Kiss Me, Dudley' or of Ian Fleming (which is brilliantly satirised by the films). The difference is that Fleming's amiable folk-tales are fiction : they take place in a meticulously documented nowhere which existed only in Fleming's curious imagination. I would not recommend the 'James Bond' books, but I would not proscribe them either. They tend, like most such novels, to proscribe themselves by quickly seeming quaint and dated. Certainly there are aspects of these books which are deeply offensive to many people, notably Bond's treatment of women as items of equipment to be used or discarded as required. Our hero is emotionally illiterate. But even the sexual idiocy and the sadism are so totally divorced from reality that indignation is not called for : the whole performance is too obviously absurd. The hilarious films of James Bond's adventures are extra-ordinarily faithful to the way they are read even by children who are 'too young for them'—with delight in all kinds of illicit pleasures, but with a vital element of credulity withheld. As a rule they are a harmless indulgence of commonplace daydreams, whereas Lord Russell's books, however well-intentioned, have a non-fictional, documentary realism which can function as pornography.

This is one reason for devoting a whole book to stories. It needs no apology, but here is one good reason. It is customary to think of 'pornography' as consisting of brutalising fictions, but real stories (and Fleming's books are real stories, not a series of stimuli threaded on a narrative) can be a means of release in which the appetites as well as the fears of our fantasy life are at worst harmlessly gratified, at best confronted and understood. The pornography of fact is much more dangerous: it has the power to break down our protective sense of unreality, to stimulate active cruelty in a few, and passive callousness in many. The greatest purveyor of pornography in our time is the camera. Yet despite the degree of realism they allow themselves, our newspapers and television are still reticent about depicting such vicious cruelties as are commonplace in myths, fairy-tales, nursery rhymes, and other forms of story, where they provide a means of growing and learning, and coming to terms with pain.

In thinking of 'good' books for children, then, it is fair to discriminate between various kinds of pleasure. Those which positively make for moral and emotional growth, which play on a child's sensitivities without leaving scar-tissue behind—these are the ones we can value most. The brutality of fairy-tales is usually of this kind, and to take an example from a book for older readers, so is the scourging of Beric in Rosemary Sutcliff's *Outcast*—a reticent but suggestive episode which is placed fair and square in a total moral system and cannot be extracted from it. Stories which are a straightforward appeal to fantasy-life and wish-fulfilment, but leave the personality at root untouched (and these are likely to be the majority of stories that any child reads) give no reason for alarm. Stories, or non-fictional works, which generate an excessive interest in abnormal sexuality or violence, or tend in any other way to halt or divert emotional development—these are the books or papers which justify forms of censorship.

In my view this is much the most important single criterion that we can use in assessing a book for children. For the adolescent reader in particular, books which 'positively make for moral and emotional growth' obviously include many which were first published for adults, and deserve to be widely-known by teenage readers. In the chapter on adolescent reading I have deliberately concentrated on a smaller but important group of books: those which are published with a teenage readership in mind, but could just as well be read by adults. There is an overlap here: Joyce Cary's *Charley is my Darling*, a novel for *adults* about the problems of delinquent adolescence, is in many ways a less intelligent, sensitive, and, incidentally, less funny novel than K M Peyton's *Pennington's Seventeenth Summer*, a novel for *adolescents* about the problems of delinquent adolescence. Both, however, are potentially enriching experiences for fifteen-year-olds, and enjoyable too. In the following pages this broad principle, 'for growth and for enjoyment', will be carried over into the commentary on individual books and authors, and into the book-lists.

Within this general criterion there are other, more specific principles that we need to decide about. There are books 'for children', sometimes written with profound intelligence and imagination, which do not observe a proper reticence in their probing of sensitive areas (see the discussion of *Finn's Folly*, pp. 88–89). It is the function of a good children's book to set foot in unexplored country, to push back the boundaries of what a child knows and understands and bring him face to face with painful or strenuous experience. It is *not* the function of such books to put the stars out and take the compass away. It is possible to be too relentless, too savagely honest in writing for children and for adolescents, exposing so many frightening possibilities, so much potential for isolation and loss, that the effect is to deepen half-felt insecurities. If there is one ethical principle that I would wish to pronounce for children's writers it is this: they should not depict situations in which emotional destitution is overwhelmingly sudden or overwhelmingly complete; whatever anguish is depicted, there must be enough light to steer by.

Some writers would complain that this involves an intolerable artistic compromise. The fact that such a complaint might be made is a good thing. It shows a reluctance to consider writing for children as a patronising activity, or as something different from other kinds of writing. One compromise, and only one, is needed: the writer must not deprive his readers of the *minimum* emotional shelter that he would regard as needful in daily life for a child of his own. One has only to remember how raw and

23

strange and disturbing a story can be, and the precaution becomes, I think, self-evidently necessary.

Some people worry about the expression in children's books of certain attitudes which they find offensive. There are, for example, racial attitudes in the 'Biggles' books, and also in works of an altogether different calibre such as *Prester John* or *Kim*, which are acutely distasteful for many parents and teachers nowadays. On this point I think it is useful to distinguish between two kinds of book: the one which contains certain assumptions because they are part of the intellectual climate in which it was written, and those which deliberately set out to propagate obsolete or repugnant doctrines. We should be very wary of turning our backs on the first of these. All of us, after all, have minds which are shaped by historical circumstance, and so did our grandfathers. Turning our backs on history is perilously close to rewriting it. *Prester John* contains attitudes towards black people which we now prefer to reject, though they are still widely held; but they are part of the world from which the novel grew, and in my experience are readily accepted as such by young readers. Children should not be protected from their past: they should be helped to understand and accept it without apology. *Kim*, apart from being a fine novel, perhaps assembles the virtues and vices of the British imperial past as fairly and vividly as one could wish.

On the other hand, the book which does not simply incorporate doctrines, but sets out to propagate them, should be treated with suspicion, and if necessary rejected. Our difficulty here is that all such stories deserve the same caustic treatment, whether we view their contents with distaste or approval.

The fact is that the whole question of propaganda and didacticism in children's books is extremely difficult. There is an element of concealed teaching, of some kind or other, in the least doctrinal story, and there is no way of excluding it. Children's fiction is an admirable source of evidence for the social historian, because it is possible to see in these books a generation's feelings for its young, its hopes and wishes for them, and the values of its own day which it most strongly wishes to transmit. The mere existence of a major literature for children is an index of society's value and concern, which fluctuates from one period to another. It is beyond denial that children are respected as individuals far more than they used to be, as we can see not only in parental attitudes but in the rapid evolution of school organisation, especially in the junior schools. The wealth of modern children's literature is another pointer to the change. Since the last war we have had a 'golden age' of children's literature, and its existence has to do with our changing sense of what children deserve and can accept. We should not take for granted the remarkable fact that so many outstanding writers have found it worthwhile to write with children in mind, or to publish in the 'juvenile market'.

The finer the literature, the more powerful its weight of 'concealed teaching' is likely to be : it is there not in obvious moral conclusions but in the imaginative shape and coherence of a story. I hope to give one account of this process in the chapter on adolescent reading, by looking at several writers' treatment of developing sexuality—a treatment which in recent years has become more daring, and also much more subtle, reflecting increasing confidence in readers.

The distinction to keep in mind, then, is that between the blatantly didactic book, which can be offensive and is rarely good, and the book which is more subtly didactic by virtue of its sheer imaginative range and power. In this respect non-fiction has also moved forward. Julius Lester's *To Be A Slave* (Longman Young Books) is a really outstanding example of an explosively emotive subject treated with a movingly subdued compassion, all the more compelling for its lack of stridency. Didacticism and propaganda, like most other things, are good or bad depending on how they are done.

Although it would be wrong, I think, to ignore the handful of precautions that we can sensibly take to ensure that children's reading does not actually harm them—and for practical purposes this usually means excluding certain publications aimed at immature adults—on the whole we can afford to be fairly unworried. In this section I have suggested some of the points which distinguish the 'good' children's book most sharply from poorer material, and there are others which we could readily add. As well as being a vivid and coherent imaginative experience, the best books will have strong, clear plotting and good narrative organisation; credible and interesting characterisation which avoids mere stereotypes (human or animal!); they will have settings which are presented with economy and easily visualised, but not surrounded by those over-elaborate 'descriptions' which children feel some public obligation to admire; they will have an individuality of 'total style', a conjunction of subject and language which is distinctive and unique; and they will have some kind of significance beyond the obvious, something related to that quality of obscurer importance which also distinguishes a first-rate novel for adults. This sounds a great deal to ask, and certainly it is not a set of qualities which children will daily require. But we have more books of this quality than we have any right to deserve, and in the following chapters and the book-lists I have selected a number—very varied in nature—which seem to me to reach very high standards without sacrificing their width of appeal.

The most important point of all is this: the 'good' book for children is, in the last analysis, the book which is right for the individual child at a particular point in time. Ideally, it will extend his experience both of life and of language a little beyond what they were before, but not present him with too tough a challenge. It will satisfy interests he already has, so that he approaches it with a willing energy of attention, but it will deepen and widen his interests too. It will, in short, be a true and attractive compromise between the familiar and the new.

How should we provide it?

Children come across books in a relatively small number of places: in public libraries, at school, and at home. Ideally, that is. In practice many children come across books only at school, so the right library conditions in the school are probably the most important single item in creating a public of habitual readers. These conditions are the concern of parents and teachers

26

alike, and they are one matter on which interested parents should never be hesitant about making a fuss. The two things that matter are the amount of money available and the way it is spent.

The first of these is very much in the hands of the local authority, and it varies substantially from area to area. Parents' and teachers' organisations in areas where expenditure on books is below the national average should wage unremitting war on the literary Scrooges who deprive their children. But everywhere the purchase of books needs to be increased, and parents should be on the watch to ensure that money for books is not being diverted to the acquisition of prestigious and costly but under-used technological equipment.

However, teachers themselves have a fair amount of choice in the way they spend, and their ideologies differ sharply. Without seeking to convert those who think otherwise, I can only report that the schools which seem most conspicuously successful in encouraging reading are those where some or (preferably) all of these amenities occur: class libraries; a central library with informal access; a policy of buying single copies rather than sets; readiness to buy paperbacks, and tolerate greater wastage for the sake of greater range; and a place in the curriculum for private reading. Of all these I would single out the class library as the crucial factor. It usually consists of a few shelves, mainly of paperbacks, which children are allowed to use informally during certain lessons or when they have completed a piece of work. The success of the class library is part of a general experience— where books are a normal and informal part of a child's surroundings, the likelihood of his becoming an addictive reader is much increased.

Teachers and parents should naturally encourage children to make use of public libraries. Here again one finds extremes of view, of the kind I mentioned earlier. Some librarians feel that their job is to meet popular demand, others that they have a duty to use their influence and buying power to disseminate 'better' books. Most libraries compromise sensibly enough between these extremes. Common sense, however, is not the good

27

librarian's only asset. The staff of many children's libraries have outstanding knowledge of their stock, and of children's literature in general, and it is far too little used by the public who vaguely categorise the librarian's task as stamping books and collecting fines. In many towns there is a librarian whose expertise on children's books is far beyond what most parents and teachers have a chance to acquire, and he could be consulted, or invited to mount exhibitions and give talks to schools, far more generously than he usually is.

And the parent? This is the most important job of all, because the constant reinforcing influence of the home is vital in determining the success of teachers and librarians, whose professional concern is reading. The argument of this chapter has implicitly described a strategy for parents—one of good-humoured, uninsistent, unsystematic and habitual interest and encouragement. It means buying books, as far as one's means allow—and often at the child's prompting, even if it does mean yet another horse on the bookshelf. (If you're lucky, or adroit, the book in question may be Mary Treadgold's *We Couldn't Leave Dinah*, or Primrose Cummings' *Four Rode Home*, or K M Peyton's *Fly-by-Night*, all of which are worth a place on anyone's bookshelf.) Actually *possessing* books is an important factor in finding *lasting* satisfaction from them, and all children should be encouraged to build up their own libraries, on however small a scale. Parents, like teachers, now have the advantage of a substantial paperback market, from which an attractive collection can be built up inexpensively.

Browsing around the children's section in a bookshop is a wholly admirable way of spending time, and parents who become really interested may well find themselves sneaking in *without* their children. The specialist bookshops are an indispensable addition to the children's book section of nationwide stationers, whose stock of hardbacks is often poor and small (although their paperback selections are frequently excellent). After all, the hardback does have its place, and at least now and again every child should have a chance to own an item from the exceptionally beautiful range of modern children's publishing.

This kind of habitual supportive interest from a parent may be the basis of a child's lifelong reading pleasure. The rest will follow. Only one less obvious point needs to be emphasised. Reading aloud to children, which sustains their interest before they can read for themselves, should not be promptly abandoned when they can. Being read to remains a pleasure long afterwards. The parent who continues to read aloud may later have to endure being read to; later still he may enjoy it; later still, he may even need it.

From these beginnings there is much more help to which parents now have access which can make the business of choosing books for children not only easy but enjoyable: the list of sources for such help is given at the end of the book, and they will add further suggestions to the book-lists given here, which are designed to form a reliable nucleus for collections in the home or the school.

C.B.F.C.—C

2 Consumer Reactions

'I'm not going to read any more books. They rot your brains.'
(Junior Boy)

This section records some observations about books and reading by a number of children and young people, mostly aged between ten and fifteen. Some are obviously highly individual, but many of them reflect widespread views.

'Most books, I think, are boring or not exciting at all.' Sadly, the eleven-year-old girl who felt this is by no means alone: she is voicing the views of many children for whom books have simply failed to work. This book is written in the belief that if we try hard enough, and take enough pleasure in the trying, as parents and teachers we can reduce the number of children who commit themselves to such unknowing self-denial. At the moment the number is huge.

For children who do like books, Enid Blyton (who is commonly believed to be male) enjoys overwhelming popularity among boys and girls alike. Julie, aged eleven, likes Enid Blyton's books 'because I like the mystery and excitement in them and the way she can carry on keeping you interested all the way through the book', and she speaks for most readers. Adventure, excitement and suspense ('they're all exciting and full of pranks') are virtues freely accorded to her. So is realism; and even when approval is qualified ('Enid Blyton books aren't realistic, but you can imagine them') there is some indication of her success—that is, the adventures have a 'just-possible' quality which can disarm scepticism. Of course, applause is not unanimous—across the whole age-range there are those who admit to enjoying Blyton 'when I was younger', but one suspects that they include some for whom this enjoyable youth is only a few hours distant, and likely to return. Praise of Blyton 'because she wrote stories for the young and older people' is not so much a comment on the actual range of her work as on its strangely persistent appeal. Outright criticism usually concerns her tone ('babyish' and 'snobbish' are the most frequent complaints), her plots ('they're all alike and boring') and her dialogue ('the Enid Blyton style—"Goody, we'll go out and pick some black-berries!" ').

Julie's approval of the Blyton capacity to sustain interest contrasts sharply with the disappointing failure of interest that many children feel about other authors, and there is some unanimity about the reasons they give. 'Loads and loads of conversation'; 'the adventure starts half way through the book'; 'the start of stories always bore me and I nearly throw them down'; 'I can't stand books with a long-winded beginning'; 'things just go on and on'. Over-extensive conversation excites special disapprobation : 'Conversation where you don't know who's speaking, like "What?", "Yes, I mean it", "Well?" ' (This particular thirteen-year-old has my full sympathy.)

On the other hand, the Blyton habit of exalting children and belittling adults is not, it seems, a stratagem which is generally popular. Books which are '*just* about children' quickly lose their appeal once the secondary school is reached, and there is short shrift for 'children who take the law into their own hands', and 'children going on adventures, coming into great danger, and—of course!—escaping unhurt'.

The heroic adventures of super-children are not the only things to incur general displeasure. Romantic love-affairs ('soppy things in a good book'; 'love stories and suchlike unexciting rubbish') encounter the most extreme resistance, even amongst older girls. Other widespread nuisances were summed up in one girl's dislike for 'hospitals and hockey'. Here and there a girl enthused on books about nursing, but in general the young reader's assessment of hospital excitements seems more accurate than most adults'! Sporty stories are often rejected, but there is a strong demand, especially from girls, for more stories in which swimming is important. Ponies and riding, of course, form a whole category of their own, and tend to elicit either besotted delight or snorting dismissal—'nothing but bloody horses!'

The everyday world and domestic life are a bit of a bore to many, who condemn 'books that have too much family life in', or 'just ordinary people's life instead of bloodthirsty books'. Some of the dissatisfaction is perhaps expressed by the girl who had 'read all Susan Coolidge's "Katy" books. I like the way she portrays REAL family life, not chocolate-box stuff.'

Inconsistency, it seems, is a tactical error for authors. (This again is where Blyton scores; she is *never* inconsistent.) The following are representative complaints. 'I don't like some stories because they sometimes start all funny at first and then go serious at the end.' 'In some books the beginnings are very boyish and then later on in the book the story gets very girlish.' 'I don't like it when there's a good war story and suddenly something daft happens like the soldiers start dancing and singing.'

On the other hand, the desire to *learn* something from a story seems to be, for the secondary school pupil, more than just a vague sense of duty : there is a real pleasure is getting two things for the price of one! '*Cue For Treason* is a great story which tells you a lot about the Elizabethans and also gives you a good adventure.' (Of course the real satisfactions occurred in reverse order, but I believe him.) '*The Silver Sword* was good because it was exciting and I didn't know a lot about the war and that told me a lot.'

If you ask children who their favourite authors are, some bizarre groupings emerge. Sometimes, of course, they arise from a sense of obligation, or because the child does not actually *know* of any authors ('Enid Blyton, Shakespeare and Billy Wright'). Sometimes an odd man out has mysteriously entered an otherwise compact set of interests ('Henry Treece, Rosemary Sutcliff, Ronald Welch, Frank Richards, Leon Garfield'). Sometimes the names reflect that extraordinary span of co-existent interests that I have noted elsewhere, and although some such groupings are no doubt bogus, they do occur with remarkable frequency. Here is a sample: 'Enid Blyton, K M Peyton and John Steinbeck'; 'Gavin Maxwell, A A Milne and Rosemary Sutcliff'; 'Michael Bond, Elizabeth Goudge and Richard Gordon'. Occasionally, the names are a reassuring delight, indicating just the kind of adventurous, free-ranging interest that we should most encourage. One of these is the following, from a twelve-year-old girl: 'René Guillot, Penelope Farmer, Malcolm Saville, Paul Gallico, Noel Streatfeild, Elizabeth Goudge, Conan Doyle'. The range of interest (or lack of sure guidance) is also suggested by the girl who had recently been reading *My Naughty Little Sister's Friend*, and *To Kill a Mockingbird*.

Apart from Enid Blyton, there was no one author of outstanding dominance. Those who came closest were Jules Verne, whose survival-value seems outstanding, J R R Tolkien, whose books were mentioned with extraordinary affection ('I like Tolkien because he made me feel sad when I was supposed to. I liked the way he described pleasure too. The book had a warm feeling to it.') and K M Peyton, who of all contemporary writers seems closest to combining high literary quality and mass appeal.

Other popular authors receive their mixed dues of laurel and sackcloth. John Rowe Townsend, for instance, not only reaps popularity from *The Intruder*'s television success, but is widely enjoyed by younger readers for *Gumble's Yard* (or *Bungle's Yard*, as one child has it). 'I like *Gumble's Yard* because it is a story that could have happened' is a characteristic opinion. But not everyone agrees. '*Widdershins Crescent* was too much like *Gumble's Yard*,' says one eleven-year-old caustically, 'all shouting and the father and Doris everlastingly drinking.' Alan Garner got some precociously literate approval from a twelve-year-old: 'He writes interesting books, with beautiful imaginative descriptions. His characters, however improbable, seem real and alive. There is always a good story throughout the book.' Another reader expressed more equivocal approval: 'My favourite books. They are magical and mysterious, and occasionally make me feel sick.' A third was rather more direct: 'It was all daft.'

At any rate, however tough the struggle may be at times, and however we may seem outgunned by the sports pages or the comics and magazines, there is hope yet, as this eleven-year-old girl may convince us: 'I would rather read books any time, because most papers have pictures of NUDES in.'

Part Two

NOTE ON USING THE BOOK-LISTS

Before using the book-lists which follow certain chapters, please read the notes below.

Selection

Each list contains approximately 100 titles. The selection is of course largely a subjective one—I have chosen books and authors, for the most part, because I admire them. But the overriding aim of the lists is to represent the range and variety of children's fiction, and to include examples of first-rate books in all the main areas to which a young reader's interests are likely to turn. To do this, while at the same time confining the lists to manageable length, has inevitably meant omitting a great many books, and a number of authors, of whom I think highly. Omissions do *not* therefore imply disapproval; they only mean that I have chosen other authors to represent the same kind of book.

Arrangement

The simplest—and least useful—way of arranging the book-lists would have been alphabetical. I have completely disregarded this arrangement in order to sub-divide the lists in other ways which seemed appropriate or interesting. Many such sub-divisions are explained during the lists, or in a note preceding them; others are self-explanatory. Where the reason for the order is not clear, it is usually because a pair or group of books have overlapping interests or are likely to have simultaneous appeal. Authors can be tracked down through the index.

Availability

Almost without exception, the books listed are in print and readily available at the time of compilation. In a very few cases I have listed an out-of-print book because it is a work of exceptional quality which is still obtainable through libraries, or is likely to be reprinted in the near future.

Again with negligible exceptions, the books listed are hardbacks. This does not indicate any prejudice against paperbacks on my part—far from it. But the relative lifetimes of hardbacks and paperbacks differ greatly. A hardback usually remains in print for a considerable time, and once it has gone out of print it can still be traced through libraries for several more years. A paperback edition, on the other hand, may be exhausted quite rapidly.

Almost all the books listed here should therefore be traceable without great difficulty for some years. Many of them are currently in paperback editions also, and many more will certainly become so in future. For example, Maurice Sendak's *Where the Wild Things Are* and Pat Hutchins' *Rosie's Walk* are currently available in reduced-size editions as Picture Puffins, and offer excellent value.

It is always worth finding out whether the book you want is currently obtainable in paperback, and your bookseller will be able to tell you. If the particular book is not in paperback, others by the same author probably are : most authors are represented in these lists by only a sample of their work.

Paperback series

For some years Puffin Story Books had the paperback market almost to themselves. This is no longer true, and some formidable competitors have emerged in the last few years. Nevertheless, under the brilliant editorship of Kaye Webb, Puffins continue to offer incomparable value—the selection of books for the series is outstandingly imaginative, the production neat and attractive, the prices very reasonable. Their publicity is also excellent, and their public relations far more than mere sales gimmickry. Membership of the Puffin Club is well worthwhile for young readers.

Other series to look for include 'Armada' books (Collins), 'Piccolo' Books (Pan Books), 'Zebra' Books (Evans), 'Storychair' books for children up to eight, and 'Carousel' books for over-eights (Transworld Publishers), and 'Knight' books (Brockhampton Press). This last series is classified by a simple colour-coding—'Red Knights' are good stories for children under ten, and 'Black Knights' for children of ten plus. 'Green Knights' are books of popular fiction, much less demanding.

Oxford University Press and Faber and Faber, in particular, issue their own paperbacks in a rather larger format than is usual for specialist paperback publishers. The work of Kenneth Grahame and A A Milne is available in paperbacks from Methuen, and of Kipling in paperbacks from Macmillan.

Prices

The book-lists include no prices, for the saddest and most obvious of reasons. In no time at all they would be out of date.

Suitability for particular age-groups

Books appear in the lists for the age-group I think most generally likely to enjoy them. This, as I have stressed in the text, is a hazardous procedure because it takes no account of the enormous range of responses in individual children. The same is true of guidance offered by publishers themselves. It is worth checking to see what age-group a publisher has in mind for a particular book, and this may appear in a very simple or a more elaborate form. The simple form is a straightforward age-indication (e.g. 9+) on the dust-covers. The elaborated form is a letter-and-number code in which the numbers refer to reading ability and the letters to estimated range of interest. The code is as follows :

Reading ability	*Age-groups likely to be interested in the book*
1. Children under six	a Children under six
2. Children of six to eight	b Children of six to eight
3. Children of eight to ten	c Children of eight to ten
4. Children of ten and over	d Children of ten to twelve
	e Children of twelve and over

Thus, a book classified 2abc requires a reading ability normally possessed by a child of six to eight, but is likely to interest many children below and above this age.

This system, used by a number of publishers, is a useful effort towards precision, but it is no more foolproof than any other against the varied tastes and whims of individuals. *All* such estimates should be treated as no more than a preliminary guideline.

In most cases books are listed here in accordance with publishers' estimates, but where I believe these to be mistaken I have not hesitated to reject them. Parents who are interested in this problem may like to look at some difficult cases and form their own conclusions : two such cases are Russell Hoban's *The Sea-Thing Child* (Gollancz) and Rosemary Sutcliff's *The Lantern Bearers* (Oxford).

3 The Pre-school Child :
Flowers in the Carpet

Mothers of young children run the gauntlet of advice as an occupational hazard, and there can be few who escape advice which is contradictory. Small wonder that so many of them come to think of each stage of their pre-school responsibilities as beset with crucial decisions at every turn.

Luckily the question of books and stories is not a complicated one, and the essential guidelines are few and straightforward. They are also important, of course : the years up to five are the ones when many parents have no professional support at all, and even when nursery facilities exist the role of the home is still vitally necessary. It is widely recognised that by the time a child goes to school a vast amount of crucial learning has already occurred, or failed to, and that a set of pre-dispositions, expectations and skills have developed to varying degrees, with consequences that will probably have a lasting effect on personality and school performance. This currently widespread truth seems enough to justify acute parental alarm, and so it would if some other sides of the matter were not more reassuring.

The most comforting of all, perhaps, is that *choice* of books and stories is rather less important at this stage than it is at later ones; it is only important at all if the total range is severely limited. We are likely to face a demand for stories which is easy enough to satisfy. Many parents enjoy satisfying it out of their own heads, making up stories for themselves, and it is well-known that several children's classics, including *The Wind in the Willows* and *Winnie-the-Pooh*, were first told in this way. But for parents whose own inventive powers are stunted by fatigue or modesty, there is plenty of other material at hand. Some of it will be in their own memories recollected from childhood, and further inexhaustible supplies are stored in print. What matters most is not that we should choose the 'right' stories to tell, because if there ever is such a thing as the 'right' story we shall only stumble on it by pure chance, but that we should be *asked* for stories, and storytelling become an accepted, customary pleasure in the young child's routine.

In the vast majority of cases the demand for stories comes almost of its own accord, although the age at which demand becomes insistent (occurring, for instance, at such unseemly hours as four in the morning) will vary widely between one child and another. If it does not come at all, there are likely to be other behavioural abnormalities of a more conspicuous kind which suggest that the child may in some way be disturbed. But in general the very normality of the whole proceeding is its chief delight. Stories are one important way in which the young child satisfies his curiosity about the world he is entering, begins to get some sense of his own identity and how it compares with other people's, begins the long process of generalising from the data of his own daily experience. At this stage there is obviously no difference in kind between hearing stories and other ways of 'finding things out'. One of the contentions underlying this book is that there remains no such fundamental difference—fiction of various kinds continues into adult life as one of many ways in which we acquire knowledge, experience and skill, but because it also becomes identified with entertainment and hence with frivolity, we lose sight of its usefulness and link it solely with leisure. The view that learning is, or often can be, inherently pleasurable has still to be fully accepted, and consequently stories come to be regarded as idle relaxations. So one hears many self-denying adults proclaim with pride that they never read novels, 'only biographies' (that is, stories which have the official merit of being partially true). At least, however, we can avoid foisting this distinction on young children since at their age it is obviously false. There are, perhaps, a few present-day households where there are well-meaning parents who might agree with Dickens's character Mr Gradgrind in his advice to the young:

'You must discard the word Fancy altogether. You have nothing to do with it . . . You don't walk upon flowers in fact; you cannot be allowed to walk upon flowers in carpets.'

In such households one might expect to find few stories, but plenty of factually-based alphabets and educational construction kits. However, I doubt if there are many such places, or many infants to tolerate them. Fancy, as Mr Gradgrind discovered, is not so easily extinguished. Instead, our purpose should be to nourish it, as far as possible to feed on demand with a profusion of stories, and walk upon flowers in every carpet.

A young child's reaction to individual stories is completely unpredictable. Again there is a rough parallel with other early developments, when children have habits and routines of their own devising which do not always fit the convenience of parents. The story one enjoyed as a small child oneself may produce yawns or floods of tears in one's own child. The story which appears wholly innocent, or indeed replete with mirth, may cause unaccountable alarm or sorrow. The story which appears brutal and bloodthirsty and downright frightening may give rise to brays of callous merriment. Last week there may have been a sure favourite, which had already withstood a number of night-fall repetitions, and this week the same story may make the child cry, or trouble his dreams: as parents we are very unlikely ever to know what has made the difference, and turned delight into anxiety. There is absolutely no way of guarding against these things—they will happen, however careful we might try to be, and the only sound course is matter-of-fact acceptance of the child's reaction, and a quick replacement of offending stories. The worst thing we can do is to seem upset or hurt ourselves, as if we were some indignant rejected author, or to probe for reasons and explanations where there are probably none to give. Of course there will *be* reasons and explanations, but rarely of a kind to which the child can give conscious expression.

If some reasons are forthcoming, then they are probably

rooted in very recent events, or else in some important phase of insecurity. For example, stories of lost children or animals, who after many adventures are reunited with their distraught mummies and daddies, will be enjoyed by most children at some stage or other. But it is quite likely that at some point the child will discover that there is no universal law which insists on such reunions—he may have been adrift for a bit too long in the supermarket, crying between the baked beans and the washing-powder, or he may have found a dead fledgling by the roadside. Whatever the cause, we shall find that for a time at least such stories are no longer acceptable, and we must turn to something else, if possible something which offers positive re-assurance, until the child has come to terms with his discovery. By and large there is a set level of tolerance which determines the amount of new experience that each child can assimilate at his present stage. It differs vastly from child to child, and also in the individual child at one time or another. We cannot predict it, but we shall be told soon enough when we have crossed it.

In the case of books which the child looks at as you read, pictures will obviously carry much importance. At first there will be, in all likelihood, many books in which a sparse, clear text —consisting only of hundreds or even tens of words—runs along-side a series of powerful and vivid pictures. These may often seem likely to frighten or disturb the child, and make us feel that whether or not we can predict his responses there is no point in actually looking for trouble. Such a book is Maurice Sendak's *Where the Wild Things Are*, in which a small boy is whisked away from his bedroom at home and goes on a strange, dream-like journey, through time, or space, or some extra dimension which is not quite either, and comes to the place where the wild things live. The wild things are drawn by Sendak with marvel-lous skill and power : their size is awesome and their appearance ferocious, yet there is also a touch of winning absurdity about them which takes the edge off their power to frighten. Neverthe-less there are many adults who feel that such monsters have no place in a small child's picture-book, and that the sheer scale of the artist's talent disqualifies him from writing or painting for the young.

There may indeed be some children whose imagination would be seized a little too compulsively by *Where the Wild Things Are*, but this is the kind of book where the risk is well worth taking. Even if children do not need to be systematically exposed

Where the Wild Things Are by Maurice Sendak

to what is 'good', they do need to come across it sometimes, and Sendak's pictorial work must be reckoned good by any standards: his tone and colour are strong and varied, but quite without garishness, his drawing vibrantly energetic, and his pictures have an imaginative wholeness which achieves continuity of style between the most everyday domestic scenes and the outer reaches of goblinesque fantasy. There is pleasure and

44

reassurance for the child in this continuity itself: turning the page, he may be startled by some newly astonishing spectacle, but he is not plunged into something nightmarishly strange and uncontrolled. Hints of the comic, hints of the familiar and domestic, are there in the wildest scenes.

That control belongs also to the child-hero of *Where the Wild Things Are* who, far from being menaced by his weird companions, attains a kind of masterful control over them and under the protection of this rule joins with them in bizarre, frenzied jollity. In this part of the story a sophisticated adult reader can see if he wishes a small allegory of the crucial, repeated childhood experience whereby dominion is established over things that were initially frightening. If this is indeed the subliminal effect of the story, no child will be the worse for it.

Like the events themselves, and the pictorial style, the brief story also works for both excitement and reassurance. Its pattern is the 'adventurous journey and safe return'—the small boy ends where he began, in his own bedroom, and his supper is waiting. This pattern is one of the simplest and most fundamental in all fiction, and we meet it here in a concise, stripped-down form, told with delightful symmetry and repetition, taking the imagination on a round trip which is both exciting and comforting. In a field where there are so few rules and so little to be sure about, *Where the Wild Things Are* can at least claim to have abundant qualities which children like, underpinned by sane and enterprising attitudes towards its readership. The book gives some very useful indications of the sort of thing to look for.

Much the same format as Sendak's—a series of powerful illustrations joined by a clear, sparse text—is used by Charles Keeping in a book which seems likely to produce the opposite effect. In this book, which is called *Through the Window*, the small boy does not leave home on any wild excursions; he stays behind his own four walls and peeps at the real world outside. He sees first of all a series of apparently disconnected people and objects, including brewery dray-horses and a queer old woman with her dog. Then the horses bolt, and everyone in the street is caught up in a single excitement. As the horses dis-

45

appear, the excitement passes beyond the small child's range of vision. Finally the horses return, quietened, and so does the old woman, who is carrying her dog. The book closes with the question in the child's own mind: why is the old woman carrying her dog like that? No explicit answers are given—none can be, because we only know what the child actually saw, through the window.

The true and likely answer to this question is obviously an upsetting and indeed horrific one. It is not an answer we shall be keen to give to an over-sensitive child, particularly one whose present sympathy for animals may be more abundant than for people. But however probable one gruesome explanation may appear, the options are left open: the book ends with a question, not a statement, and parents reading this story with their children can easily invent more innocent explanations if the true one seems dangerous. In confronting his small child-witness with the real world, ruling out make-believe, Keeping has taken a risk, and he has compounded it by leaving the child helpless and bewildered. There is none of the assured mastery achieved by the child in *Where the Wild Things Are*. But with great tact and delicacy Keeping has also left it open to us to avoid the extremes of his realism if we need to. And since the worst possibilities suggested by the story arise directly from the text, there is no harm in a child just looking at the pictures—by doing so he can invent all kinds of stories to explain what he sees.

The particular merit of this excellent story lies in the remarkable interaction between the illustrations and the story. In a few concise sentences Keeping suggests the curiosity, the sharp observation, the quickening interest and the puzzlement of his young subject, and the illustrations are totally in harmony with the text. Above all, the positioning of the curtain, and the amount of it which is visible at any one time, is an exact pointer to the direction and intentness of the child's gaze. It is all done with extraordinary skill.

In Keeping's book the brief text raises possibilities which are not directly suggested by the illustrations. The opposite effect is achieved with great skill and visual wit in Pat Hutchins' *Rosie's*

Walk. Rosie is a hen, and the very brief text recounts her constitutional around the farmyard—a circular tour which ultimately brings her back to her own coop. There is no mention in the words of another presence in the farmyard which is highly conspicuous in the pictures—a fox. As Rosie, all unknowing and unperturbed, strolls forth in dignity, the hunting fox pursues her. Every time we turn a page and find some words which tell us where Rosie is, the fox is ready to pounce. When we turn the

Rosie's Walk by Pat Hutchins

next page there are no words at all—only the results of the fox's leap. And the results, for the fox, are a series of comic and humiliating disasters. He is deluged with water, smothered in flour, carried off by a runaway cart, attacked by angry bees— and meanwhile Rosie, all oblivious, marches on to home and safety.

This colourful and amusing story is full of visual inventiveness and energy. In the brilliant stylised drawings Rosie, while

47

discernibly a true hen, also has the posture and carriage of an unruffled matron, while the sinuous fox is alive with anticipatory laughter, which makes it all the funnier that the laugh is always, and raucously, on him. The experience offered by this story is clearly very different from that of *Through the Window* : here it is the pictures which present the extra possibilities which the words omit, so that the child is, so to speak, let into a narrative secret as he hears the story read, and the effect is comic, not disturbing. The essential point, however, remains the same : words and pictures interact to produce a strong, unified and original experience. Children who like *Rosie's Walk* will probably enjoy, a little later, the same author's *Tom and Sam*, in which the same pictorial energy is linked with a rather longer and more demanding story.

In all these books, of course, author and illustrator are one and the same person, but their work does suggest a kind of ideal for such picture-stories for the young. The primary effect is visual, as it should be : but the story as a sequence of *words* is not given a mere perfunctory, inferior place. On the contrary, what needs to be emphasised about all the books is the sheer quality of the writing—the quality of the illustrations is obvious enough, but what is not perhaps so obvious is the amount of clear, vivid, uncluttered narrative which is compressed into a few short sentences.

Not all the pictures that the young child will find and like in his books have the distinction of Sendak or Keeping, and they do not need to. A great deal of distinguished work is available, such as the splendid illustrations by Brian Wildsmith which can give to traditional stories a new surge of brilliant life, but there is also much poor or indifferent art-work in books for small children. No matter : we cannot be connoisseurs all the time, not even at the responsible age of three, and provided that something of the best modern work comes the child's way (for keeps, of course) the over-literal, over-garish or otherwise inferior pictures in other books will do no damage. It is just as well that this is so, since the child is certain to come across such inferior work, notably in the mass of books and pamphlets which are derived from poor television and film cartoon series. We cannot insulate the child from such material, but we can submerge it in the sheer plenitude and variety of pictures which come his way. Pictures, pictures everywhere is the ideal. It is important that they should be good, but still more important that they should be plentiful.

Unfortunately production costs continue rising, and picture books are expensive. There is, perhaps, a great temptation for parents to buy a few, carefully selected books of recognised excellence, or to go for several thick volumes which seem to offer bulk rewards for the money spent, rather than to buy a lot of books which, however attractive, seem limited in scope and unlikely to last. There is also a temptation (easily justified by the plea that children must 'learn how to value nice things') to put these lovely and costly items on a safe, high shelf, and get them out at story-time. One is bound to sympathise with the urge, and often the necessity, to treat books in this way. But, if we can possibly bring ourselves to it, we ought to face the fact that the small child's books, some at least of which will be among the most beautifully produced that he will ever own, are also the most expendable. Their destiny is fingermarks and tearing, gratuitous extra decoration and broken spines, and in the end the rubbish bin. We cannot expect small children to parcel out their enthusiasm into sessions of careful, supervised page-turning. The more popular a book, the more quickly it will fall to pieces. But the experience of repeatedly handling a well-liked picture book, and enjoying the freehold on it so that it can be produced at will, is an educative pleasure in itself, and one which ought not to be denied. If the ultimate result is ruin, the book will not for that reason have been wasted : far from it.

However much we should like young children to have, there are severe limits on the amount most parents can afford to spend. If it is right to reconcile ourselves from time to time to the spectacle of a valuable book in shreds, it is obviously sensible to take full advantage of the cheaper things available. 'Paperbacks' for the very young can be surprisingly durable (the miniature books concerning Dougal and other personages from the BBC's

Magic Roundabout seem especially resistant to violence) and they certainly pay their way. The publishers of the 'Ladybird' series have deserved their success by, amongst other reasons, producing books which are remarkably tough little hardbacks. Their quality in other respects is variable, but often quite excellent, and the series is first-class value for money. So the wisest policy is to buy as plentifully as one can, using the extensive range of cheaper books but also taking care to purchase, occasionally at least, the kind of book in which a good printer has done justice to a good artist—the kind of book which by its very nature cannot be cheap. Having done that, the most difficult thing of all is perhaps to allow the child to treat this book like the others, but this is nevertheless exactly what we should do.

Some books and stories, first acquired when the child is very small, will continue to hold his affections for a number of years —quite possibly well after he has started school. Such progression as we can observe is likely to be very erratic, but it will broadly consist of a gradually increasing number of narrative words which can be supported by a single picture. As a general rule the pre-school child needs stories in which there is one picture for every incident : it is too much at this stage to expect that a child will be able to follow a series of incidents without any regular visual support. But the *complexity* of events the child can understand will rapidly develop, and with this complexity will come the need for a longer accompanying text; what happens is that the words elaborate more fully on the picture, not that they form a substitute for it. This calls for some delicacy of judgement, and it is here that the remarkable skills of Beatrix Potter come into their own. One of the numerous virtues of Miss Potter's work is her unerring sense of balance between her language and her pictures : she knew exactly what would work at any given stage of a story. Because she is so justly famous, it is almost certain that some of her books will come the child's way, so the general recommendations of this chapter should perhaps focus for a moment on her work in particular. Graham Greene wrote a splendid satirical essay ('Beatrix Potter', in *The Lost Childhood and Other Essays*) in which he compared the phases of her artistic development with those of Shakespeare. There is a real truth in this dexterous piece of comedy: Beatrix Potter's work is much more varied than its standard format suggests, and not only are some of her books more linguistically demanding than others, but some exhibit a streak of icy ruthlessness, a merciless sang-froid in matters of life and death, which can upset and deter young children considerably—far more than the mass of fairy-tales and nursery rhymes which might seem more obviously frightening. She is not a 'safe' classic, a distinction which does belong, among others, to A A Milne. The 'Pooh' stories really are a permanent storehouse of fun for the year or so before school starts; but with the formidable Potter we need to pick and choose.

Enough has been said, I hope, to suggest the sheer expansiveness and range of this period of growth—its multiple possibilities and its unnerving lack of rules. All we can do is to go on experimenting ourselves, and letting the children do so. They will sometimes want stories which are purely domestic (like the 'My Naughty Little Sister' stories) and sometimes they will want the wildest fantasies. We can expect them to get a lot of pleasure from rhyme, and it would be wrong to end this chapter without insisting again on the importance of traditional nursery rhymes. Sometimes, perhaps, they will pause for a quiescent phase in which they do not want stories at all. We need to be prepared for anything, including a good deal of pleasure for ourselves, and we need always to keep in mind that we are watching a miraculously rapid awakening of life and experience, remarkable for its sheer intensity. It is worth remembering the words of Alison Uttley, herself the provider of so much pleasure for children, at the opening of her essay 'The Weaving of Fairy Tales':

'In childhood, whether this is the childhood of the human race or the primitive childhood of early man, everything is new with vivid life. This personification of inanimate matter is called "imagination", but it is deeper than the senses, it is a real knowledge of a secret of the Universe, the flux of living and dying, the eternal change of living atoms, and the vital spark which is present in all matter.'

(*Secret Places and Other Essays*, Faber & Faber)

Meal One by Ivor Cutler, illustrated by Helen Oxenbury

BOOK-LIST FOR THE PRE-SCHOOL CHILD

(See the note on pp. 37–39 and also some books listed under 'Classics')

Maurice Sendak	*Alligators All Around*	Collins
	Chicken Soup with Rice	
	Pierre	
	One Was Johnny	

A set of miniature books—an alphabet, a counting book, a story and a book of the months—published as a set entitled 'The Nutshell Library'.

Some alphabets:

Celestino Piatti	*An Animal ABC*	Benn
Brian Wildsmith	*ABC*	Oxford
Helen Oxenbury	*ABC of Things*	Heinemann
George Adamson	*A Finding Alphabet*	Faber
John Burningham	*ABC*	Cape
Rodney Peppé	*The Alphabet Book*	Kestrel
Dick Bruna	*B is for Bear*	Methuen
Dr Seuss	*Dr Seuss's ABC*	Collins
Susanna Gretz	*teddybears ABC*	Benn

John Burningham's *ABC* is specially recommended, but it is a good idea to let small children look at several, and notice connections for themselves. The same applies to:

Some counting books:

Brian Wildsmith	*123*	Oxford
George Adamson	*Finding 1 to 10*	Faber
Helen Oxenbury	*Numbers of Things*	Heinemann
Susanna Gretz	*teddybears 1 to 10*	Benn
Rodney Peppé	*Circus Numbers*	Kestrel
Dean Hay	*Now I Can Count*	Collins

Now I Can Count also gives specific help on learning to tell the time, which is also the subject of

Peggy Blakely	*Anna's Day*	A & C Black

Two more things to know about:

Dick Bruna	*My Vest Is White*	Methuen

a help with the business of colours.

Beman Lord	*The Days of the Week*	Angus & Robertson

Some stories in pictures without words:

Renate Meyer	*Hide-and-Seek*	Bodley Head
Ruth Carroll	*What Whiskers Did*	Collins
Peter Wezel	*The Good Bird Nepomuk*	Wheaton

Fernando Krahn	*How Santa Claus Had a Long and Difficult Journey Delivering His Presents*	Kestrel
	A Flying Saucer Full of Spaghetti	
Paul Shardlow	*The Mayor's Table*	Kestrel
Iela Mari	*The Magic Balloon*	Angus & Robertson
John S Goodall	*Jacko*	
	Paddy's Evening Out	Macmillan
Lilo Fromm	*Muffel and Plums*	Hamish Hamilton
Pat Hutchins	*Changes, Changes*	Bodley Head

Changes, Changes has good bold pictures illustrating what useful articles can be constructed from a pile of wooden blocks. A good example of the negligible difference, for the very small, between stories and creative play.

Christmas matters:

| Reinhard Herrmann | *The Christmas Story* | Macmillan |
| Dick Bruna | *The Christmas Book* | Methuen |

Two re-tellings of the Christmas story, that by Dick Bruna for the very youngest children.

| Jean de Brunhoff | *Babar and Father Christmas* | Methuen |
| Brian Wildsmith | *The Twelve Days of Christmas* | Oxford |

the traditional story beautifully re-told in pictures.
See also Fernando Krahn's book earlier in the list.

Elizabeth and Gerald Rose	*Good King Wenceslas*	Faber
Masahiro Kasuya	*Long ago in Bethlehem*	A & C Black
Raymond Briggs	*Father Christmas*	Hamish Hamilton

Nursery Rhymes and Fairy Tales:

Raymond Briggs	*The Mother Goose Treasury*	Hamish Hamilton
Brian Wildsmith	*Mother Goose*	Oxford
Hilda Boswell	*Treasury of Nursery Rhymes*	Collins
James Orchard Halliwell	*The Nursery Rhymes of England*	Bodley Head
Iona and Peter Opie	*The Oxford Nursery Rhyme Book*	Oxford
Beatrix Potter	*Appley Dapply's Nursery Rhymes*	Warne
	Cecily Parsley's Nursery Rhymes	
Raymond Briggs and Virginia Haviland	*The Fairy Tale Treasury*	Hamish Hamilton
Hilda Boswell	*Treasury of Fairy Tales*	Collins
Barbara Sleigh	*North of Nowhere*	
Helen Cresswell	*At the Stroke of Midnight*	
Raymond Briggs	*Fee-Fi-Fo-Fum*	Hamish Hamilton

Brian Wildsmith	*The Owl and the Woodpecker*	Oxford
	The Hare and the Tortoise	
Nicholas Tucker	*Mother Goose Lost*	Hamish Hamilton
C S Evans	*Cinderella*	Heinemann
	The Sleeping Beauty	

For some collections and adaptations of the Brothers Grimm and of Hans Andersen, see the book-list on 'Classics' (pp. 131–132).

Some collections of stories:

Eileen Colwell	*The Youngest Storybook*	Bodley Head
	Tell Me A Story	Penguin
	Tell Me Another Story	
	Time For A Story	
Norah Montgomerie	*To Read and to Tell*	Bodley Head
	More Stories to Read and to Tell	

includes 2-minute stories for reading at bedtime.

Barbara Ireson	*The Faber Book of Nursery Stories*	Faber
Dorothy Edwards	*The Read to Me Story Book*	Methuen
Sara and Stephen Corrin	*Stories for Under-Fives*	Faber

For young television addicts:

Eric Thompson	*The Adventures of Dougal*	Brockhampton
	Dougal's Scottish Holiday	
	Misadventures of Dougal	
	Dougal Round the World	
John Ryan	*Captain Pugwash*	Bodley Head
	Pugwash Aloft	
	Pugwash and the Ghost Ship	
Oliver Postgate and Peter Firmin	*Nogbad and the Elephants*	Kaye & Ward
Elisabeth Beresford	*The Wandering Wombles,* etc.	Benn

Other book-versions of famous television series are also available, but the above are some of the very best. Listeners with Mother will probably also enjoy:

| Dorothy Edwards | *My Naughty Little Sister,* etc. | Methuen |

Deservedly popular series:

Edward Ardizzone	'The Tim Books'— e.g. *Tim All Alone*	Oxford
Diana Ross	'The Little Red Engine'— e.g. *The Little Red Engine Goes to Market*	Faber
Rev W Awdry	'Railway Series'— e.g. *Four Little Engines*	Kaye & Ward

Dick Bruna	'Miffy' books—	Methuen
	e.g. *Miffy at the Seaside*	
Dr Seuss	'Dr Seuss Books'—	Collins
	e.g. *Mr Brown Can Moo, Can You?*	

See other titles in the Collins' series 'Beginning Beginner Books', and, for slightly older children, 'Beginner Books'.

| Jean and | 'Topsy and Tim' books— | Blackie |
| Gareth Adamson | e.g. *Topsy and Tim's Monday Book* | |

From this series, it is worth taking special notice of

Topsy and Tim Go Safely

which is about crossing the road, and

Topsy and Tim Take No Risks

which is about safety in the home.

Several mice:

Graham Oakley	*The Church Mouse*	Macmillan
John Yeoman and Quentin Blake	*Mouse Trouble*	Hamish Hamilton
Don Freeman	*Norman the Doorman*	Brockhampton

A choice of other picture-stories:

| Michael Bond and Fred Banbery | *Paddington Bear* *Paddington's Garden* | Collins |

The first titles in a new series of 'Paddington' books for the pre-school child.

| Barbara Softly | *Ponder and William at the Weekend* | Kestrel |

The teddy-bear world, attractively presented.

Edward Ardizzone	*Nicholas and the Fast Moving Diesel* *Peter the Wanderer*	Oxford
	Paul the Hero of the Fire *Sarah and Simon and No Red Paint*	Kestrel
James Reeves and Edward Ardizzone	*Titus in Trouble* *The Angel and the Donkey*	Bodley Head Hamish Hamilton
Gareth Adamson	*Old Man Up a Tree*	Abelard-Schuman
Quentin Blake	*Jack and Nancy*	Cape
Hans Baumann	*Fenny*	Abelard-Schuman
Kenneth McLeish	*Chicken Licken*	Kestrel
V H Drummond	*The Flying Postman*	
Nicholas Brennan	*Jasper and the Giant*	
Russell Hoban	*Bedtime for Frances* *A Baby Sister for Frances*	Faber

Victor G Ambrus	*The Sultan's Bath*	Oxford
	Hot Water For Boris	
Pat Hutchins	*Rosie's Walk*	Bodley Head
Michael and Joanne Cole	*Kate and Sam Go Out*	Methuen
Charles Keeping	*Alfie and the Ferryboat*	Oxford
	Charlie, Charlotte and the Golden Canary	
	Through the Window	
	The Spider's Web	
Maurice Sendak	*Where the Wild Things Are*	Bodley Head
	In the Night Kitchen	
	Hector Protector and As I Went Over the Water	

Two indispensables:

A A Milne (illus. E H Shepard)	*Winnie-the-Pooh*	Methuen
	The House at Pooh Corner	
	When We Were Very Young	
	Now We Are Six	

and

| Beatrix Potter | | Warne |

The difficulties presented by this most excellent and prickly genius are referred to in this chapter. The stories are grouped below as follows: one that is specially suitable to start with, partly because of the extreme brevity of its text; a number which are generally suitable for pre-school children; and four which are best reserved until the others have been read. Some are omitted from this pre-school list entirely, and included in the list for the next chapter.

Beatrix Potter	*The Story of a Fierce Bad Rabbit*	Warne
	The Tale of Two Bad Mice	
	The Tale of Mrs Tiggy-Winkle	
	The Tale of Mr Jeremy Fisher	
	The Tale of Tom Kitten	
	The Tale of Mrs Tittlemouse	
	The Tale of Timmy Tiptoes	
	The Tale of Ginger and Pickles	
	The Tale of Peter Rabbit	
	The Tale of Squirrel Nutkin	
	The Tailor of Gloucester	
	The Tale of Jemima Puddleduck	

Starting school:

| Shirley Hughes | *Lucy and Tom go to School* | Gollancz |
| Alison Prince | *Joe and the Nursery School* | Methuen |

4 The First Years at School:
Neighbours and Strangers

Despite the increasing tendency to graduate the introduction of school experience by means of play-groups and nursery classes, going to school 'properly' at the age of five is still a momentous step in a child's growth. Sometimes parents are inclined to inflate its significance by expecting—and trying to promote—swift advancements in their children's tastes in stories. 'When I went to school I put away childish things' is more true in parental desire than in reality.

During these first three or four years of school it is true that for most children remarkable developments will occur. But for some time they are likely to take the form of additions and extensions to a store of experience which the child brings with him, rather than sudden rejection of pre-school favourites. Children will still like, and need, books which are chiefly picture-books, and they will still want to hear old stories repeated, or to practise new-found reading skills on them. Bedtime stories in particular are likely to be nostalgic occasions, when the child can halt the need to assimilate new experience and return to familiar ground.

The kind of story that children enjoy may seem to change little for a time, but we shall notice a growing readiness for stories which are longer, depend on a more even balance between text and pictures, and are less episodic in their plots. For example, in the chapter on pre-school books we saw in Maurice Sendak's *Where The Wild Things Are* a fine example of one standard theme and structure for the children's story—the 'adventurous journey and safe return'. This formula, which is popular because it answers to a deep-laid interest and is capable of almost endless variations, will be found to recur in books for all age-groups. At three, the child may like Maurice Sendak's book, which despite its supposedly fearsome pictures is fundamentally reassuring in form. At six or seven, the same child may equally well enjoy Helen Cresswell's *Where The Wind Blows*, a short but more developed story in which there is not only a move from pictorial to verbal priority, but also a plot in which the fresh air blows more crisply and the reassurance is not quite so marked. It is quite likely that a child will enjoy both at once, taking on the more elaborate story while still retaining his enjoyment of Sendak's pictures (if they have managed to survive the destructive potential of the years between!).

The same kind of process takes place very commonly with animal stories. A A Milne's classic 'Pooh' stories will be heard with pleasure by three- and four-year-olds. Michael Bond's superb 'Paddington' stories, however, are not likely to appeal strongly to most children until they are about six. There are several likely reasons for this. Although the two fictitious bears have certain things in common, including a kind of insane common sense which repeatedly lands them in scrapes, there are some respects in which the Paddington excursions are more demanding. Paddington books are just as episodic as Pooh stories, but the episodes tend to be longer and more intricate, depending on a more extended series of hilarious causes-and-effects : consequently the full humour of the plot demands rather more stamina to be completely appreciated. The incidental humour of the Paddington stories is also more sophisticated, deriving its point from the manifest oddities of the human adult world, especially those adults who are so foolish as to think it surprising that human tasks should be performed by bears. The world of grown-ups is not actually deflated in Pooh, except by remote control through certain animal-equivalents, but in the Paddington stories satire is more directly aimed at various adult 'types', and children need a year or two of additional experience before this comedy is fully meaningful to them. Here there is another likely sequence : the child who enjoys Pooh before starting school will probably enjoy Paddington soon afterwards —but he can also achieve the geographical feat of arriving at Paddington without first needing to desert Pooh Corner.

There are other qualities which we can expect children to like in their early school years. Some of them can be clearly seen in Helen Morgan's story *Mrs Pinny and the Blowing Day*. Mrs Pinny, an engine driver's wife, takes in washing for several families, and when it is finished she delivers it to her clients in an old black pram. But on one such day, when the washing-day wind has been more trying that usual, it completes its day's misdeeds by lifting Mrs Pinny and her pram high into the air above the railway-line, and blowing her through the sky:

'Below her, the smoking snake of the four thirty-six chugged cheerfully down to Bunbridge.

A soldier, a nurse, and a little fat man happened to glance out of the windows as the pram flew by in the sky.

The fat little man fell right off his seat, the soldier snorted and shut his eyes and the nurse made a noise like a nightmare.

Then the soldier put his head out of the window and shouted and the nurse put her head out of the window and screamed and the fat little man just sat on the floor and held his head in his hands.

Windows went clattering down on their straps, passengers woke from their nice little naps, some cheered and some jeered and some waved their caps and some of them yelled for help.

Then one of them PULLED THE COMMUNICATION CORD!

Such a thing had never happened before when Mr Pinny was driving. He was not just perplexed, he was quite clearly vexed as he brought the train to a stop.'

The most noticeable thing about this writing is its sheer verbal extravagance, the Dylan Thomas-like intoxication with words which makes it read like a junior *Under Milk Wood*. The alliteration, the frequent internal rhymes, the tricks of style which make the book a halfway house between comic prose and comic poetry—these things can be quite exasperating for adult readers, so it is vital to recognise that many young children thoroughly enjoy them. They are a natural development from the early language-games of pre-school times, and they sustain a delight in the inventive possibilities of language. The adult reader may recoil from such extravagance, but 'the road of excess', said Blake, 'leads to the palace of wisdom'.

We also need to notice that these quasi-poetic techniques are used for comic purposes—the absurd lyrical momentum of events is abruptly broken by the sudden prosaic line which records the dramatic but sternly commonsense, anti-climactic act of pulling the communication cord. In short, the language has not gone mad; it is under tightly-organised comic control.

The book as a whole displays the qualities suggested by this bizarre episode. It is usually rooted firmly in everyday routine —Mrs Pinny's meticulous washing procedures are described in much detail. It has a steady eye for human foibles, especially when people's behaviour is infected by the boisterous, purpose-less energy of the wind. It shifts from familiar domestic detail to the wildest flights (literally) of fancy, and does so with surprising suddenness. If it is junior Dylan Thomas one moment, it is junior Gwyn Thomas the next. And the whole result forms a most successful piece of writing for children at the infant-school stage to hear read, and for children a little older to read for themselves—a delightful blend of truth and fancy, poetry and wit. Most important of all, its success derives largely from its indulgence of stylistic trickery which adults are likely to find particularly irritating, and from that we need to take due warning.

At this stage of reading, when children are beginning to strike out on their own, established favourites like Alison Uttley's 'Sam Pig' books will also have their place, not to mention those tales of Beatrix Potter which, although originally intended for younger children, sometimes depend on fearsome and ruthless plotting which is most appreciated at about six years old. The next stage will probably bring in more of the 'little people', in one guise or another. In 'BB's *The Little Grey Men* we meet gnomes who inhabit, not a world of pure fantasy, but a realistically drawn countryside in which the small figures take on vivid life. Other

61

The Little Grey Men by 'BB', illustrated by
Denys Watkins-Pitchford

little people whose company should not be missed are Mary Norton's 'Borrowers'. The outstanding skill of both 'BB' and Mary Norton lies in creating a finely imagined miniature world, in which the scale and proportionate size of things are conveyed with sharply observant accuracy and the precision of a watch-maker's eye. Mary Norton's books in particular deserve more attention than there is space for here. Their achievement is not only one of visual imagination : it is also one of carefully con-trolled feeling, in that she depicts a dwindling and precarious society teetering on the very edge of survival, but never allows her stories to slip over the edge into moods of acute distress. The 'Borrowers', with their quaint, serious ethics and their oddly complete, endangered way of life, are likely to be for many children an early encounter with stories which work on more than one level of meaning.

During the first two or three years at school, children will, of course, need to have most such stories read aloud to them. They are for the most part far too difficult for beginner-readers to read for themselves. Stories which children *can* manage at the early stages of reading are also widely available, and they are likely to include some favourites left over from the pre-school years. Amongst the many new stories we can give to them when they start to read, Hamish Hamilton's series of 'Gazelle' books, intended for the five- to eight-year-olds, are worth special men-tion : the stories are good, and the demands of the language particularly well-judged. By looking at books in this series we can accurately gauge what kind of book it is appropriate to give, and the same publisher's 'Antelope' books, intended for seven-to nine-year-olds, include many excellent stories for the next phase of reading development. As the age-range itself suggests, progress naturally varies considerably from child to child, and for many young readers the 'Antelope' series is quite difficult enough. For many others, however, reading development is much more rapid, and the rest of this chapter is concerned with books that are quite within the compass of quicker readers by the age of nine or ten.

Amongst them is another series which, like the 'Borrowers'

books, can be read at several levels of meaning—the celebrated 'Narnia' series by C S Lewis. These are often read in the upper reaches of the junior school, by children of nine onwards, and although their readership obviously extends to older children it seems right to consider them here. The 'Narnia' books are allegories, in which beneath the surface adventures the Christian story is re-told.

Few books for children in recent years have won so much fame as the chronicles of Narnia. Narnia is a country to which the children of our own world, the 'sons of Adam and daughters of Eve', are allowed occasional entry, and in which they take on princely stature and rescue the land from evils. They do this at the behest and under the guidance of the great lion Aslan, the Christ-figure of the stories, the divine beast who creates and destroys, who is sacrificed and rises from death, who can bring peace or terror.

The whole project of this series is ambitious and challenging, nothing less than a major Christian allegory presented through the children's adventure story. It is no criticism to say that the underlying Christian doctrine escapes the notice of many young readers; it is a function of allegory that it can be read with full understanding at different strata of insight, and the series is both popular with children and admired by adult critics.

Admiration is not, however, unanimous, and the opposite view was expressed at its most forthright by Alan Garner, who once described the books as technically inept and morally vile. Even if one does not accept that criticism completely, it is possible to see it as a useful corrective to the general enthusiasm and admit that it has some truth.

One of the greatest mistakes, in my view, is to see the Narnia books as representing a consistent body of work, all intellectually and theologically consistent and equally good as stories. This view was certainly reinforced by the award of the justly coveted Carnegie Medal to the final volume of the series, *The Last Battle*. The award was obviously intended as much for the entire series as for the individual book, but it was nevertheless an unfortunate choice. *The Last Battle* is not a good novel, and is probably the weakest book in the entire seven-volume chronicle : its weakness as a story seems closely connected with the heavy allegorical load it has to carry. The following passage, which 'describes' the 'spiritual Narnia' to which the deserving characters are admitted after the 'real Narnia' has been destroyed at Doomsday, gives some idea of the book's technical deficiencies :

'It is as hard to explain how this sunlit land was different from the old Narnia as it would be to tell you how the fruits of that country taste. Perhaps you will get some idea of it if you think like this. You may have been in a room in which there was a window that looked out on a lovely bay of the sea or a green valley that wound away among mountains. And in the wall of that room opposite to the window there may have been a looking-glass. And as you turned away from the window you suddenly caught sight of that sea or that valley, all over again, in the looking-glass. And the sea in the mirror, or the valley in the mirror, were in one sense just the same as the real one yet at the same time they were some-how different—deeper, more wonderful, more like places in a story : in a story you have never heard but very much want to know. The difference between the old Narnia and the new Narnia was like that. The new one was a deeper country : every rock and flower and blade of grass looked as if it meant more. I can't describe it any better than that : if you ever get there you will know what I mean.'

If there is one thing that virtually all critics of children's literature are agreed on, it is their dislike of 'writing down' to children. Yet I know of few worse examples of 'writing down' than this passage from a greatly admired, prize-winning book. The conspicuous authorial presence and nudging, conspiratorial address to the reader, the cumbersome, distracting explanation, the final coy disclaimer of the writer's ability—all are evidence either of narrative incompetence or a patronising collusion with the child. Such writing may have its admirers; what is surprising is that it has so few critics.

One could point to other weaknesses in Lewis's writing : he is not averse to sharing a sly joke which only adults are likely to catch—at the expense of 'progressive' parents, for instance—and his plotting is sometimes clumsy. Worse than this, however, is the ambiguous nature of his god-figure, Aslan, who suddenly becomes in *The Horse and His Boy* a version of the Old Testament God of anger and retribution instead of the God of forgiveness and love. This unexplained switch is typical of moral uncertainties inherent in the chronicle. This is not to say that the series as a whole is poor, only that it is very uneven. *The Horse and His Boy* and *The Last Battle* (which in any case is inexplicable unless you have read earlier books) are for various reasons open to serious objections. *The Magician's Nephew* (in my view easily the best book in the series), *The Silver Chair* (which contains Lewis's most delightful and memorable character, the marsh-wiggle Puddleglum) and *The Voyage of the Dawn Treader* are all, if somewhat overpraised, nevertheless very good reading. But the chronicle as a whole does not have the coherence and mastery which are often attributed to it.

If C S Lewis's work has perhaps been overvalued, there are two other writers whose work is specially appropriate for children of nine or so, and who have not yet been as widely recognised as they deserve. They are Mollie Hunter and Helen Cresswell.

Mollie Hunter's stories are compact and economically-told, with a vigorous narrative energy that compresses much incident into a tale of about a hundred pages. They draw heavily on Scottish and Irish folk-lore, and specialise in confrontations between strong-minded modern characters and intruders from the world of magic. The results are often very funny, sometimes serious or sad. A fine example of Mollie Hunter's work is the simply told and beautifully constructed novel *Patrick Kentigern Keenan*, which is a model of first-rate writing for older juniors. Patrick Kentigern Keenan is a boisterous and attractively conceited Irish gentleman who believes himself to be 'the smartest man in all Ireland'. Proving one's claim to such a title is a hazardous business, since it involves taking on the little people, and Patrick finds himself involved in several chastening adventures. By his attempts to outsmart the fairies he incurs a good deal of discomfort and ridicule, but his sobering experiences never quite extinguish his boastful claim—one day, he is determined, his fellow-Irishmen will acknowledge it for true. And sure enough, one day they do. In his early adventures Patrick regularly loses face or suffers humiliating discomforts, yet each time his household is somehow enriched by a trophy won from fairyland; in the last adventure all his treasures save one are lost, and the one that remains he has earned for himself, but this is also the adventure in which by his ingenuity and courage he makes good his boast, and deservedly wins the praise he has struggled for. Perhaps this gives some idea of the perfect shaping of the story : it is broken up into a series of incidents, each of them a stirring yarn in its own right, but with each episode the story as a whole moves forward, leaving Patrick richer both in treasure and in inner strength, and consequently more prepared to face his last great test. Technically, therefore, the book is extremely accomplished—episodic yet unified, combining separate excitements with overall meaning, and told without a word wasted. Moreover, the development of the story is matched with the developing wisdom of Patrick's character in a way that children readily notice and appreciate.

Even better, in my view, is another of Mollie Hunter's books in which she draws from Scottish folk-lore : *The Kelpie's Pearls*. It is an exciting, amusing, oddly wistful story which is made especially powerful by its moving portrait of a lonely, practical and very determined old Scottish lady, caught up inescapably in a web of magic which takes away from her the precious simplicities of her secluded life. This too is an admirable book— lightly and crisply told, amusing and shrewd, but playing with great delicacy on much deeper chords of feeling.

Helen Cresswell writes excellent stories for younger children, such as *Where The Wind Blows*, which was mentioned earlier in this chapter. Her best work, however, is written for children of roughly nine or ten. These books, of much the same scale as Mollie Hunter's, have some of the same delightful qualities : they are packed, eventful stories told with economy and skill; they are unfailingly inventive and original; they are full of humour and gaiety as well as excitement, but they touch on deeper human truths with warmth and understanding. Technically too, these writers have a basic method in common. Helen Cresswell's novels often comprise a series of exciting and to some degree self-sufficient incidents, but connected by a strong narrative impetus. They carry their readers forward without depending simply on the need to know 'what happens next'. In fact like so many of the outstanding books for children, they are very good stories, but also something more, a widening of human experience.

The Signposters is a book which shows Helen Cresswell's work at its most relaxed and gay. Taking as its starting-point the ubiquitous surname 'Smith', the story explains in light-hearted fantasy how the clan came to be so widely scattered. One itinerant family, a branch of the Flockshire Smiths, has the job of touring the country repairing signposts, and they are struck by the happy notion of using their travels to organise a massive reunion of all the Smiths in Flockshire. This simple but original picaresque formula is the basis of a delightful story, in which a lively sequence of places, incidents and characters reaches its climax in the triumphant reunion itself.

In sharp contrast to *The Signposters* is *The Night-Watchmen*. Here there are more itinerants, the tramps Caleb and Josh, but they come from a place where surnames are unknown, and which can only be reached by whistling up a mysterious 'night train'. This remarkable novel is full of humour—the tramps are choosy about their bedding ('Nothing like *The Times* for warmth, and not so easy to come by every day of the week'), they cover up their strange activities by digging holes in the road and erecting a watchman's hut beside them ('Just dig a hole and put up a red flag and you could camp till doomsday and not a question asked'), and with their primitive facilities they cook up meals of mouth-watering splendour. But mystery and menace underlie these things : Caleb and Josh are in danger, pursued by the threatening greeneyes, human-like creatures who are blinded by daylight but can see in the dark. The place from which Caleb and Josh have come, and the train that can take them back, must somehow be kept immune from the relentless peril that dogs the tramps wherever they wander. We meet them

Thomas and the Warlock by Mollie Hunter,
illustrated by Charles Keeping

in our own ordinary world, and it is an ordinary boy who becomes entangled in their doings. *The Night-Watchmen* generates an extraordinary mixture of comedy and tension; it is both a tale of hilarious eccentricities and a gripping drama of escape and pursuit, with potential victims for whom we feel amusement and deep affection. There is nothing in modern children's literature quite like Helen Cresswell's characteristic atmosphere of comic oddity and obscure alarm, and *The Night-Watchmen* shows her remarkable gifts at their impressive best.

Finally, it is worth remembering that children between eight and ten often like what they call 'old-fashioned books'—the best children's stories from the past, such as Frances Hodgson Burnett's *The Secret Garden* and E Nesbit's *The Railway Children*. The language of such fine survivors from earlier periods is not difficult, the plots are strong and attractive, and there is an intriguing quaintness about their everyday detail which can fascinate children in this age-group, and lay the foundations of their pleasure in many other books, written or set in times past, which they will come to later on.

BOOK-LIST FOR THE FIRST YEARS AT SCHOOL

(*See the note on pp. 37–39*)

This list is divided into three general sections, the first for the five- to six-year-old age-group, the second for the seven to eight, the third for the eight to ten. Like all such categories they are rough-and-ready, and will not be a reliable guide to the tastes or abilities of any individual child. These age-groups broadly correspond to the intended readership of three series published by Hamish Hamilton—'Gazelle' books, 'Antelope' books, and 'Reindeer' books. In my view these are the liveliest and most accurately judged of available series, and each section opens with a small sample from the appropriate list, which not only includes some good stories but should give a convenient guide to the level appropriate for the 'average child' in each age-group. The 'average child', of course, is never the one you have in mind at any one time!

SECTION ONE (*5–6-year-olds*)

Janet McNeill	*A Helping Hand*	Hamish Hamilton
Noel Streatfeild	*Let's Go Coaching*	('Gazelle' books)
Elfrida Vipont	*Michael and the Dogs*	
Ursula Moray Williams	*The Good Little Christmas Tree*	
Christobel Mattingly	*The Surprise Mouse*	

Beatrix Potter in reserve: these are books which are best kept back until children are at school:

Beatrix Potter	*The Tale of Benjamin Bunny*	Warne
	The Tale of the Flopsy Bunnies	
	The Tale of Pigling Bland	

A number of Beatrix Potter's books are available in initial teaching alphabet (i.t.a.) editions. *The Tale of Squirrel Nutkin* is also available as a children's play with music arranged by Christopher le Fleming.

Alison Uttley books

Alison Uttley	*The Brown Mouse Book*	Heinemann
	'Little Grey Rabbit' books— e.g. *How Little Grey Rabbit Got Back Her Tail,* etc.	Heinemann ('Cowslip' books)
	Little Grey Rabbit's Pancake Day, etc.	Collins
	'Sam Pig' books— e.g. *Sam Pig Goes to Market,* etc.	Faber

Two collections:

Kathleen Lines (ed)	*The Ten-Minute Story Book*	Oxford
Sara and Stephen Corrin (eds)	*Stories for Six-Year-Olds and other young readers*	Faber

And some illustrated stories:

Helen Cresswell	*The Bird Fancier*	Benn
	The Sea Piper	Chatto, Boyd and Oliver
Alison Prince	*Joe Moves House*	Methuen/BBC
Alfons Weber	*Lisa Goes to Hospital*	Blackie

A story to help small children to prepare for a stay in hospital.

Edward Ardizzone	*Diana and her Rhinoceros*	Bodley Head
	Johnny's Bad Day	
	Johnny's Good Day	
Graham Greene	*The Little Train*	Bodley Head
	The Little Fire Engine	
Delia Huddy	*Sugar and Spice*	Kestrel
Celestino and Ursula Piatti	*The Little Crayfish*	Bodley Head
Oliver Postgate	*Ivor the Engine*	Abelard-Schuman
Roy Brown	*The Wapping Warrior*	Chatto, Boyd and Oliver
Aingelda Ardizzone	*The Night Ride*	Kestrel
Tamara Kitt	*Jake*	Abelard-Schuman

Jane Hollowood	'Maggie' books—	
	e.g. *Maggie and the Birthday Surprise*	Chatto, Boyd and Oliver
Margaret Howell	*The Lonely Dragon*	Kestrel
Elizabeth Borchers	*The Old Car*	Blackie

SECTION TWO (*7–8-year-olds*)

Gillian Avery	*Ellen and the Queen*	Hamish Hamilton ('Antelope' books)
Raymond Briggs	*Sledges to the Rescue*	
Eilis Dillon	*A Pony and Trap*	
Janet McNeill	*Dragons Come Home*	
Rosemary Sutcliff	*The Truce of the Games*	
Ruskin Bond	*The Blue Umbrella*	

Two collections:

| Sara and Stephen Corrin (eds) | *Stories for Seven-Year-Olds and other Young Readers* | Faber |
| Margery Fisher (ed) | *Open the Door* | Brockhampton |

Eleanor Farjeon books

Eleanor Farjeon	*Italian Peepshow*	Oxford
	Jim at the Corner	
	Kaleidoscope	
	The Little Bookroom	
	The Old Nurse's Stocking-Basket	

Varied collections of stories by a most distinguished children's writer. *The Little Bookroom* was a winner of the Library Association's Carnegie Medal.

'Moominland' books

| Tove Jansson | *Finn Family Moomintroll* | Benn |
| | *Comet in Moominland*, etc. | |

'Paddington' books

| Michael Bond | *A Bear called Paddington*, etc. | Collins |

and by the same author, 'Thursday' books about a slightly less well-known animal

| | *Here Comes Thursday*, etc. | Harrap |

'Worzel Gummidge' books

| Barbara Euphan Todd | *Worzel Gummidge at the Circus*, etc. | Evans |

The worlds of trolls, bears and scarecrows in these series are likely to be greeted affectionately by most children in this age-group. Enthusiasts for the animal creations of Michael Bond will probably also like to meet his guinea-pig in:

| Michael Bond | *The Tales of Olga da Polga* | Kestrel |
| | *Olga Meets Her Match* | |

and Maurice Sendak's Sealyham in

| Maurice Sendak | *Higglety Pigglety Pop! Or There Must Be More to Life* | Bodley Head |

More stories of animals, fairies, matters outlandish or domestic:

| Madeleine l'Engle | *Dance in the Desert* | Kestrel |

A story by a gifted writer, beautifully illustrated by Symeon Shimin.

Ted Hughes	*How the Whale Became*	Faber
	The Iron Man	
Helen Cresswell	*Where the Wind Blows*	
Philippa Pearce	*Beauty and the Beast*	Kestrel
	Mrs Cockle's Cat	
	The Squirrel Wife	
Elizabeth Goudge	*I Saw Three Ships*	Brockhampton

A delightful book by another of the older generation of children's writers, to whom their successors are mightily in debt.

| Emma Smith | *Emily's Voyage* | Macmillan |
| Russell Hoban | *The Sea-Thing Child* | Gollancz |

This is a speculative choice. Some people would argue that it is better for much younger children, others that it is not a good children's book at all. I think this is where it belongs.

Antony Maitland	*James and the Roman Silver*	Kestrel
Betty Roland	*The Forbidden Bridge*	Bodley Head
	Jamie's Summer Visitor	
Eleanor Estes	*The Witch Family*	Kestrel
Helen Morgan	'Mrs Pinny' stories— e.g. *Mrs Pinny and the Blowing Day*, etc.	Faber

See pp. 60–61. These books may also be enjoyed by rather younger children.

Helen Morgan	'Mary Kate' stories— e.g. *Meet Mary Kate*, etc.	Faber
Margaret Mahy	*The Witch in the Cherry Tree*	Dent
	Rooms to Let	
Byrd Baylor	*Coyote Cry*	World's Work
Renate Meyer	*Susie's Doll's Pram*	Bodley Head
Dorothy Clewes	*Wanted—a Grand*	Chatto and Windus

SECTION THREE (8–10-year-olds)

Charlotte Hough	*The Hampshire Pig*	Hamish Hamilton
Andre Norton	*Steel Magic*	('Reindeer' books)
Barbara Willard	*A Dog and a Half*	
'BB'	*Bill Badger and the Big Store Robbery*	
	The Little Grey Men	Methuen
	Down the Bright Stream	
	The Forest of Boland Light Railway	Brockhampton

The Little Grey Men, a classic children's book, deservedly won the Carnegie Medal. *Down the Bright Stream* is a sequel to it.

The 'Borrowers' books

Mary Norton	*The Borrowers*	Dent
	The Borrowers Afield	
	The Borrowers Afloat	
	The Borrowers Aloft	
	Poor Stainless	

Some books by Mollie Hunter:

Mollie Hunter	*The Ferlie*	Blackie
	The Kelpie's Pearls	
	Patrick Kentigern Keenan	
	Thomas and the Warlock	

Some books by Helen Cresswell:

Helen Cresswell	*The Outlanders*	Faber
	The Night-Watchmen	
	The Piemakers	
	Up The Pier	
	The Bongleweed	

Up the Pier is a good starter for children who may enjoy time-fantasies, which are listed separately after Chapter 6.

The 'Narnia' chronicles

C S Lewis	*The Magician's Nephew*	Bodley Head
	The Lion, the Witch and the Wardrobe	Bles; Collins
	The Silver Chair	
	Prince Caspian	
	*The Horse and His Boy	
	The Voyage of the Dawn Treader	
	*The Last Battle	Bodley Head

* These two books are listed for the sake of completeness, but see pp. 63–66 for comment on them.

Some other stories: from past and present, at home and abroad

René Guillot	*The Children of the Wind*	Oxford
stories of the African bush		
Rosemary Sutcliff	*Brother Dusty-Feet*	Oxford
the strolling players of long-ago England		
Armstrong Sperry	*The Boy Who Was Afraid*	Bodley Head
adventure in the South Seas		
John Rowe Townsend	*Gumble's Yard*	Hutchinson
	Pirate's Island	Oxford
adventures in modern Britain		

| Frederick Grice | *The Black Hand Gang* | |

adventure in the time of the First World War.

And a mixed bag:

Lucy M Boston	*The Sea Egg* *Nothing Said*	Faber
Betsy Byars	*The Eighteenth Emergency*	Bodley Head
Jennifer Wayne	*The Smoke in Albert's Garden*	Heinemann
Jenny Overton	*The Thirteen Days of Christmas*	Faber
Nigel Grimshaw	*Bluntstone and the Wild Keepers*	
Gillian Baxter	*Pantomime Ponies* *Save the Ponies!*	Methuen ('Pied Piper' books)
Michael Hardcastle	*In the Net*	

Ponies for the girls; football for the boys.

Clive King	*Stig of the Dump*	Hamish Hamilton
Ruth Tomalin	*The Sea Mice*	Faber
Richard Parker	*Spell Seven*	Kestrel
Nina Bawden	*On the Run*	Gollancz
Philippa Pearce	*A Dog So Small*	Kestrel
Roy Brown	*The Thunder Pool*	Abelard-Schuman
Vian Smith	*Moon in the River*	Kestrel
Eilis Dillon	*The Wild Little House*	Faber
Joan Aiken	*The Wolves of Willoughby Chase*	Cape

The last nine are introductions to a number of excellent writers, with plenty more to offer to children who enjoy their first taste. In some cases their appearance may seem premature, but they are worth trying at this age for willing readers, as of course is:

| Meindert de Jong | *The Wheel on the School*
The Tower by the Sea | Lutterworth |

Two titles as an introduction to a very popular, very able writer.

Two introductions to the much-loved 'Brer Rabbit' are

| Julius Lester | *The Knee-High Man and other tales* | Kestrel |
| David P. Makhanlall | *The Invincible Brer Anansi* | Blackie |

Finally, four titles from a very useful new series to start young readers on historical fiction, Heinemann's 'Long Ago Children Books':

Leon Garfield	*The Boy and the Monkey*	Heinemann
Jenny Seed	*The Red Dust Soldiers*	
Geoffrey Trease	*A Ship to Rome*	
Jill Paton Walsh	*The Toolmaker*	

5 From Junior School to Secondary (1): The Immediate World

In the years from ten to thirteen the child is passing through an exciting and bewildering phase of growth. A mass of new experiences, ideas and feelings have somehow to be assimilated during a short period of transition from childhood proper to the verge of adult life, and for many children these are years of tension and uncertainty which their resources of language and expression are inadequate to deal with : they cannot describe their perplexities clearly, either to themselves or others. A year or two later, in mid-adolescence, it may be much easier for the apprentice-adult to share his experiences with others, and in so doing to understand them better. This is one reason among many why the notorious 'adolescent phase' of problematic behaviour is frequently less stormy to endure, and easier for parents in particular to cope with, than the stage preceding it.

Our national arrangements for schooling have, in their wisdom, made a public institution of this tempestuous phase by implanting a change of school in the middle of it. The evils of the eleven-plus examination and the inefficient (not to say brutal) segregations it entailed are now familiar enough to the majority of teachers and parents, but the idea that a change of school at eleven is wrong in itself, whether it involves selection or not, has yet to gain a similar acceptance. Whether people will generally come to hold this view depends on the achievements of the new middle or intermediate schools, which have been introduced in many areas—often on grounds of expediency rather than principle, as a convenient means of introducing comprehensive education without needing to build new schools. But whatever the reasons for their emergence, these schools make institutional sense of the stages and processes by which children grow : they provide a homogeneous unit in which children should be able to move backwards and forwards between childhood and adolescence, without feeling that their school environment draws a clear-cut boundary between the two.

Roughly speaking, this chapter and the next are concerned with Middle School reading, and it may be helpful to think of it like that, especially in places where school transfer normally occurs at eleven. The period between the tenth and the thirteenth birthday is all of a piece, and variety is the essence of it. At this stage we can expect disconcerting shifts from one level of maturity to another, inexplicable reversals as well as abrupt developments, wild fluctuations of interests and feelings. It is the job of the Middle School to make humane provision for such exhilarating diversity, and parents as well as teachers need to provide for a similar ebbing and flowing in the choice of books.

There are, broadly speaking, two literatures for children which can particularly help them at this stage. The first is the immediately realistic, which confronts the child with situations he can readily identify himself with, and with characters or settings which are 'close to home'. This kind of book is the main subject of this chapter. The second is the literature set in remote and unfamiliar settings, the world of the is-not or the never-will-be, in which potentially disturbing experiences are placed at a distance and so become more manageable—the historical novel, the futuristic novel, and the fantasy. The next chapter covers books of this kind.

We may discover some useful guidelines in this section by looking first at a book which straddles these rough categories—Mark Twain's *Tom Sawyer*. Many books, of course, are 'realistic' in some ways and 'fantastic' in others, and the point of dividing them up is simply to sort out some of the differing but equally important qualities of each experience. No book has ever been written in which the real and the fantastic are more closely interwoven than *Tom Sawyer*, and this is my reason for borrowing it from the 'classics' chapter, to which it properly belongs.

77

It is because *Tom Sawyer* can never quite decide what kind of book it is, because it moves so fluidly between escapist daydream and bitter realities, that it is one of the great classics of the transitional phase between childhood and maturity.

The events that occur in *Tom Sawyer* include these: Tom conducts a highly successful swindle; he plays truant from school; he runs away from home and sets up a secret encampment on an uninhabited island; he makes a dramatic return to civilisation by confronting the grief-stricken adult populace at his own funeral; he teases and outwits a number of adults; he witnesses a murder at dead of night, and is instrumental in exposing the murderer; he 'finds' buried treasure; he pictures himself in numerous romantic adult occupations, such as piracy and theft; he gets lost in a dangerous place, together with another child who depends on him, and saves both their lives by his own efforts and courage. Huckleberry Finn, besides assisting in some of these enterprises, saves the Widow Douglas and in turn becomes a public hero.

When events like these are listed, it is clear how *commonplace* the book is. Almost every cliché of fiction for boys, almost every heroic role they play in private fantasies is contained in it somewhere. This is not in itself a weakness: commonplace plotting and stereotyped situations may be grave deficiencies in popular fiction for adults, but for children the stereotyped situation is often an important one, offering some particularly satisfying way of testing or asserting oneself at a safe distance from reality. Books which supply these situations do an honest service, and they stand or fall not by what they do but by their skill in doing it, by the colour and vividness of the life they give to clichés. In this respect *Tom Sawyer* is an immensely skilful book. In reading it the child is enticed into complicity with Tom in a number of classical fantasy situations. But the book's commitment to boyish fantasy is never wholehearted. Tom himself is presented from the outset as a romantically inclined, make-believing, superstitious character, with an above-average disposition to manipulate the world in accordance with his pet fantasies. This is made so obvious that the young reader's willing complicity with Tom is not accompanied by any illusions about the kind of boy he is. He is there to be conspired with, but also to be laughed at.

Awareness of Tom's weakness is accompanied as the book proceeds by a progressive revelation of the realities which lie in ambush for Tom's fantasy life. Often these revelations are unequivocally comic, involving the well-deserved punishment of Tom's machination and conceit. In other cases, though, the story touches sensitive nerves and explores complex emotions. The escape to Jackson's island of Tom, Joe Harper and Huck Finn is a particularly fine example of excellent writing for children at this phase of development; in a broad setting of comic fantasy which is reassuring, it explores at several levels of realism and seriousness the implications of the boys' romantic disappearance and its actual consequences for themselves and others.

Some of the events in this stirring episode simply depict boastful pretension smartly followed by poetic justice. Tom's and Joe's first attempts at smoking have enjoyably predictable results. At other times we find that the dream-world is merging disturbingly with the actual, and the younger reader is confronted with the outcome of his fantasies. At first the restrictive adult world is joyfully repudiated, and the freedom of isolation generally enjoyed, but as time passes and novelty wears off, there is an unromantic and unexpected consequence: homesickness. Tom and Joe are forced as a matter of honour to vie with each other in concealing or disguising this unpiratical emotion, especially in the presence of Huck Finn, who has no domestic ties to draw him homeward. But the emotion is real, and the more painful because of the codes which demand that it should be hidden. This lurking occurrence of realism, intruding into the fulfilment of fantasy and romance, is characteristic not only of the Jackson's Island episode but of the book as a whole, and partly explains its wonderfully delicate balance between the culmination of childhood and the early stages of mature awareness. At a stage of growth where such primary fantasies are regarded by the child with mingled affection and disenchantment, indulgence

79

and shame, the book sounds familiar discords, and performs one of the most valuable functions that a book can fulfil at any stage of a child's development (and of the adult reader's for that matter). It enables him to see the puzzling disharmonies of his own personality in an objective and enjoyably reassuring form and recognise that they are not unique.

Tom Sawyer would not be so important a children's book if this pattern—of movement from dream to reality, from wish-fulfilment to disillusion—occurred with didactic regularity throughout the book. It is no business of the children's writer to engage in the systematic spoliation of dreams and the destruction of myths. The achievement of the book is its characteristic ebb-and-flow, its continual reminders that attempts to enact fantasies often go wrong, and its frequent confirmation that sometimes they go triumphantly right.

The culmination of the Jackson's Island episode (when Tom, Joe and Huck, all believed by a grieving community to have drowned, make a sudden and dramatic reappearance at their own funeral) is an outstanding example of the book's occasional reminders that fantasy does not always end in disillusionment. The occasion is a triumphant success for Tom, granting all he could wish in the way of theatrical effect. A whole series of delinquencies have led to this moment, but condemnation of them is overlaid by the joy which the people of St Petersburg feel at recovering their lost ones. This outburst of communal joy is repeated later in the book when Tom and Becky are recovered from their ordeal in the underground caves. St Petersburg, in many ways a crude and violent society, is true to its Bible in its treatment of prodigal sons.

Of course *Tom Sawyer* is a 'classic' (although like many classics, often misunderstood). It is familiar enough to need no advertisement, but my reason for basing the recommendations in this chapter on a detailed account of it concerns its representative quality, its generous inclusiveness of all the vagaries and inconsistencies which mark this period of child development, and its vivid rendering of the fears and shocks of growth. 'Generosity' is perhaps the key-word: Twain accepts the child-world with amusement and affection, welcoming its oddities without attempting to subject them to strong implicit judgement or censure. The point is made in an essay by the American critic Diana Trilling, where she examines the public reaction to Tom's two disappearances:

'Twice Tom disappears, in circumstances where his fault is clear, but there is no hint on the part of neighbours or friends of adverse moral judgement on his character or upbringing. Corrupt and unfeeling as the adult world of St. Petersburg may be, it retains a concept of innocence—innocent childhood and innocent parenthood—which is now gone from American life. For, whatever our present-day concern with children—and it could scarcely be greater —we now bring to any violation of the childhood norm an extraordinary readiness of moral judgement, and on parents no less than on the child. In terms of "advantages", Tom and his friends may be markedly underprivileged compared to children today— to see the difference we have only to catalogue the contents of Tom's pockets, the mad odds and ends of string and metal that make up his "worldly wealth". But Tom is accepted in all his quirkiness and error and mess as no boy today can hope to be. Indeed, the more serious the trouble in which Tom lands, the less, not the more he is blamed.

In the 1870s Twain could have no premonition of a time when the idea that "boys will be boys" would be thought morally dangerous.'

('Tom Sawyer—Delinquent' in *Claremont Essays*,
Secker & Warburg.)

Mrs Trilling is commenting here on the nature of a whole society: it is one which is much concerned with bringing up its children to be upright and self-confident and trustworthy adults, but is also ready to accept that children are often irresponsible and silly. St Petersburg is ready to accept behaviour which we are inclined nowadays to regard as anti-social. (One of the great novels about children written in modern times is John Hersey's *The Child Buyer*, which depicts within a framework of fantasy the horrific potential of attitudes towards childhood which are too preoccupied with the 'norm' of customary behaviour. It is *not* a novel for children, but it deserves to be widely read by parents and teachers.) Children in this age-group, and boys especially, are interested in books which show young people in testing situations, coping with ordeals and emerging from them stronger and more mature, but it is also important that the element of play and make-believe should not be wholly excluded. It may be that, despite the apparent permissiveness of modern society, we have a diminishing tolerance of childish or irresponsible behaviour and that this is affecting modern children's fiction. The point may become clear if we look closely at two other authors.

Tom Sawyer's world has space for growing. The scale of the river Mississippi and its surrounding countryside offers massive chances of adventure—it is the ideal adventure playground, with plenty of risks but few mishaps. Such conditions for boyhood are no longer possible for most children: the modern city-child has far fewer chances of real-life adventure than his counterpart of a century ago, and the 'adventure holiday' in its various guises is an indication of what is missing from daily childhood experience. There are not enough good novels which deal imaginatively with the realities and constraints of town life, such as those of Roy Brown. Nevertheless, one function of the children's novel is to create the living spaces which are often denied to the urban child.

This need was met by one of the founding fathers of modern children's fiction: Arthur Ransome. Ransome's books have begun to recover their popularity after a period of disfavour, and are now available as paperbacks. There are certainly some valid criticisms to be made of Ransome: his characters are rather stereotyped, and lack the psychological depth of many later novels for children. But his dialogue has passed the stage of seeming 'dated', and his plots and situations have many qualities important to the modern reader.

The predominant tone is set at the beginning of *Swallows and Amazons*, the first book in the series for which he is best known. Father, consulted at long distance about the wisdom of letting his children loose with a boat, wires back: 'Better drowned than duffers if not duffers won't drown.' Right from the outset the children carry some responsibility for their own fate—they are sailing a real boat on real water, and accidents can happen. They are expected to exercise a sound, tough common-sense, to know the rules of safety and to keep them. But in the early books there are two constant factors to mitigate the harshness of their premature independence. Mother, who is a good deal more hen-like than a modern mum should be, is never far away and keeps an unobtrusive eye on things. She belongs to that wearingly virtuous breed of fictitious parents who make themselves scarce for most of the time but promptly reappear when needed. In short, the world of adult support is voluntarily set aside, not lost. Secondly, the children themselves erect a large-scale make-believe world around their modest venturings, a world of 'enemies' and 'natives' and exotic goings-on. In such books as *Swallows and Amazons* and *Swallowdale*, in fact, we see children visibly acquiring self-reliance in a world of loosely-controlled play, filled with small-scale real adventures and vast imaginary ones. Whatever reservations one might have about the books, the formula is ideally suited to many children's tastes and needs.

There are two books in particular where Ransome abandoned his formula, in my judgement with very different results. In the absurd *Missee Lee*, the fantasy situation is permitted to become the true one, and the plot loses credibility: it is an unfortunate book, quite out of keeping with the others. The opposite happens in what I believe to be the best of all Ransome's books, *We Didn't Mean to go to Sea*. The book opens familiarly enough, with the children invited to spend a brief holiday on the yacht *Goblin*, captained by a responsible adult, while Mother clucks protectively close at hand. But disaster strikes: despite a promise to Mother that the boat will not go outside Harwich harbour, she drags her anchor in thick fog, with only the children on board. All the games of seamanship, and voyaging, and designated naval rank, suddenly take on a terrible actuality. The eldest boy John really is the captain now, with a life-or-death responsibility for his family's safety as the boat is caught first by fog and then by rain and gale. The story of *Goblin*'s voyage across the North

Sea on a night of vicious weather is excitingly told, and it is the real thing: out of all the apparatus of make-believe that the children assembled in earlier adventures, they preserve only what is needful for good discipline in a crisis, the realities of duty, obedience and command. (One of the greatest of all novels about the finding of maturity, Joseph Conrad's *The Shadow Line*, has almost identical themes: this is fundamental experience which can be reworked at many levels.)

The story loses some of its momentum towards the end—the final stage of the voyage, which takes place in calm and delight, is something of an anti-climax, and when the children make harbour at Flushing they are reunited with their father in most improbable circumstances. But there is also point and rightness in the conclusion: once *Goblin* is safe in a Dutch port, we notice that the younger boy, Roger, has again begun to use the language of earlier make-believe, while 'Captain John' becomes a child again in some ways. But *only* in some ways: his father rightly refuses to divest him entirely of his captaincy, and he is allowed to keep some of the responsibilities he has so painfully earned. The events of the night were real, and they had to be faced without adult aid. There is no going back, and having come through their ordeal successfully the crew of *Goblin*, especially the captain, can never again be children as they were. *We Didn't Mean to go to Sea* shows in a compelling way what all the adventure-play of earlier stories was really for.

In Arthur Ransome's books, then, we can see some of the same qualities that we found in *Tom Sawyer*, but with a more uncompromising drive towards self-reliance and maturity, and a closer connection between fantasy and reality, the pretended adventure and the true one. If we now turn to a much-praised children's writer of our own time, the Australian novelist Ivan Southall, we find that in his work the power to embellish experience with fantasy, or to take refuge in irresponsibility and play, are forbidden indulgences for most of the children he creates.

It is characteristic of Southall's books that they concern children whose precarious maturity is subjected to extremities

The Boy and the River by Henri Bosco,
illustrated by Lynton Lamb

of trial. In the very typical *Ash Road* we have the story of a group of boys setting out for a camping trip in (the phrase seems appropriate) the suburban bush. They do so at a time when the risk of bush fires is great, and stringent precautions are imposed on everyone entering dangerous zones. In the middle of their first night's camp, they have a minor accident which in the prevailing conditions is enough to precipitate appalling disaster.

The rest of the novel is concerned with two things. The first is the fire itself and the devastation it causes—a widening diameter of ruin which is rendered with frightening vividness of detail. In this dimension the book exists as an adventure story —as a tale of danger, uncertainty, resistance and hairsbreadth escape. In children's fiction it is not uncommon for plots to be based on natural catastrophes, or the threat of them, but what is startling about this story is the sheer scale of the phenomenon— its depiction of the familiar element, fire, in outlandish states of uncontrol. Focusing on a fairly small range of characters in a few detailed settings, Southall is able to convey the sense of a whole community at risk, and bush fire comes to represent all forms of potential natural destruction which humanity, however brave or ingenious, can scarcely hope to combat. The quality of Southall's writing is such that many young readers are caught up vividly in an imaginative experience which is exhilarating as well as terrifying: the sense of a world which is not dependable, in which one can only survive by courage, effort and exertion.

On this level the novel succeeds admirably, and it need do no more. But Southall's concerns are deeper than this, and in *Ash Road*, as generally in his novels, he engages secondly with the question of moral responsibility. The fact is that a disaster of enormous magnitude was precipitated by the momentary thoughtlessness of a group of boys, who then have the problem of facing up to what they have done. 'Boys will be boys' is no answer here, and we are not presented with a forgiving society of the kind Tom Sawyer returned to (though admittedly his escapades did not produce such comprehensive effects). For the inadvertent arsonists of *Ash Road* there is really no excuse, and we know that in the opening pages, as the boys set out on their trip, we saw them pass through a landscape of *total warning*, which is made vividly clear to us as readers. The situation in *Ash Road* is characteristic of Southall's books, and his concern for such situations makes him one of the most relentless and uncompromising of children's novelists. The fact is that *Ash Road* depicts a moral catastrophe as awesome as the physical. These boys know that they were responsible for a ruinous fire, that they should not have been, and that all the customary pleas of extenuation, like inexperience or accident, are useless : the guilt is theirs, and although it may be relieved, it must still be lived with. They are trapped by responsibility just as their community is trapped by flame.

Not many children's writers pursue such matters as rigorously as Southall does. But clearly there is a difference of major proportions between this world, and the hospitable world of *Tom Sawyer* which can so readily let fantasies exist. In both books the attractions of escape and freedom, of removal from the shelter of adult surveillance, are there, as they are there in so many books for this age-group. Such freedoms can give chances for fantasy and daydream to be happily fulfilled, or they can lead the unwary child into minefields of adult choice and responsibility.

It is here that Southall's work poses a problem. In looking at these three authors, whose work spans a century, I have not sought to suggest a widespread, consistent tendency for writers to present children with ever-bleaker issues of responsibility and guilt. Writing for children is not consistent in its assumptions, and never has been. What we should notice is the general sense of what children can fairly be asked to face, and Southall perhaps represents the extreme point of psychological demand in contemporary writing for children. Ironically, we have reached a point where a children's library may contain books which are every bit as horrific as those nineteenth-century works which Gillian Avery describes so graphically in her book *Nineteenth-Century Children*, when she shows just how morbidly 'improving' it is possible for children's books to be. It is ironical because the early Victorian works were based on a deeply pessimistic view of the child's moral nature, while Southall's work, at its most demanding, grossly overestimates the moral and psychological resilience of children. His very distinction as a writer, combined with his refusal to compromise, face us with the question of censorship.

Ash Road is both a fine novel and a legitimate book for children. Another of Southall's books, *Finn's Folly*, seems to me the kind of story from which children need to be protected. It is written with great subtlety and insight, and explores some raw and sombre truths about human experience. Why, then, should I reject it?

In my view, the choice of human experience examined in this book is likely to cause great distress to many young readers. In the cold and the dense fog of an Australian winter night, a lorry carrying chemicals jack-knifes on a hairpin bend and crashes into a gorge. The driver's daughter is with him in the cab, and he dies beside her. Before the lorry leaves the road a car hits it at speed and is crushed. In the car are the mother and father of four children who have been left in a remote holiday shack nearby. The youngest of the four brutally orphaned children is a mongoloid boy. For much of the story he is lost in the fog, wandering away in his pyjamas; he is found near a mass of cyanide spilt from the lorry, and at first is thought to be dead. The eldest of the children, Max, discovers the fog-shrouded crash and attempts to free the driver's daughter, who is trapped but unhurt; as he struggles to free her, a first, sudden onset of sexual love and need overcomes them both, only to be crushed and turned into compulsory betrayal by a sudden and cruel twist of plot. The children must face their desolation and, where it exists, their duty.

This outline by no means renders the full horror of the story, but perhaps it gives some notion of the book's remorseless concentration on matters which even an adult will find distressing, and may cause deep anxiety and anguish in a child. If the book were less accomplished it would be less dangerous, but it is a work full of honesty and truth—honesty and truth from which children should be shielded, if the act of shielding still has any meaning and justification.

It may be argued that Southall's work is written for older readers than those in this age-group, and properly belongs in a later chapter. Perhaps so, but libraries do not discriminate so finely, and books like *Finn's Folly* can be found on shelves open to quite young children. That, together with his continuing pre-occupation with a major theme for middle-school readers, seems to make this the right place to discuss him. I have distributed his books in the lists that seem appropriate for them. *Finn's Folly* will not be found in any.

Ivan Southall's more recent novel, *Josh*, was awarded the Carnegie Medal, and deservedly so. Needless to say it is another trial-by-ordeal, and it has been criticised in some quarters for much the same reasons that I have advanced against *Finn's Folly*. Certainly it contains some grim episodes, but on the whole it seems to bring a new and welcome dimension to Southall's work. There is a dry underlying humour which is not exactly conspicuous in his earlier books, and the book's perspectives shift in such a way that its young and suffering hero does not command either unreserved sympathy or outright censure. The reader can identify with Josh, yet feel enough amusement to keep his sympathy slightly at a distance: as a result the story is absorbing but not overpowering. It is a promising development in a writer of formidable gifts.

Precisely because the books discussed in this chapter are dealing with the business of becoming adult, they are difficult to classify, and it is a shared responsibility of author, publisher, reviewer, teacher and parent to make sure that in supplying an essential experience they do not overstep the mark and make unbearable demands on young readers. *Finn's Folly* is by no means the only book that should never have slipped through the net.

BOOK-LIST FOR JUNIOR SCHOOL TO SECONDARY (1)

(See the note on pp. 37–39)

Most of the novels in this list fall into the broad categories of 'adventure stories' or 'family stories'—often both—and there is little need to differentiate them. They are, almost without exception, good of their kind, and many of them follow up the crucial preoccupations outlined in this chapter. There are, however, three categories which deserve some specialised mention—stories of school, of horses and ponies, and of football:

Some school stories:

Mary Harris	*Seraphina*	Faber
	The Bus Girls	
	Penny's Way	
Antonia Forest	*Autumn Term*	
	End of Term	
Geoffrey Trease	*Under Black Banner*	Heinemann
	No Boats on Bannermere	
Elfrida Vipont	*The Lark in the Morn*	Oxford

The list is not exhaustive or exclusive, of course: it is merely a start for children who want stories with a strong school interest. None of these books is solely a school story, and other books listed below deal in part with school life. And mention should perhaps be made of Anthony Buckeridge's 'Jennings', a popular and honourable descendant of the 'comic school story' tradition.

Some football stories:

Michael Hardcastle	*Goal!*	Heinemann
	Shoot on Sight	
	Soccer is also a Game	
	Goals in the Air	
Bill Naughton	*The Goalkeeper's Revenge and other stories*	Brockhampton

A book of short stories, in which only the short but masterly title-story has an exclusively football interest. The other stories, however, are also very popular with young readers.

Robert Bateman	*Young Footballer*	Kestrel
Brian Glanville	*Goalkeepers are Different*	Hamish Hamilton

The last two titles are semi-documentary, and Brian Glanville's book, the work of a gifted writer for adults, blends fact and fiction, real and imaginary characters and clubs, in a slightly uncomfortable way which may soon cause it to seem dated. But it is a useful contribution to a subject where demand exceeds supply.

Some stories of horses and ponies:

Mary Treadgold	*We Couldn't Leave Dinah*	Cape
	No Ponies	
	The Heron Ride	

	Return to the Heron	
K M Peyton	Fly by Night	Oxford
Primrose	Four Rode Home	Dent
Cumming	Wish For A Pony	
Monica Edwards	Cargo of Horses	Collins
Catherine Cookson	The Nipper	Macdonald
Katharine Hull	The Far-Distant Oxus	Cape
and		
Pamela Whitlock		

An amusing skit on the conventional pony-story is

C Northcote	Ponies Plot	John Murray
Parkinson		

Older readers in this age-group should also be recommended to look at the novels of Vian Smith, and at K M Peyton's *Flambards*.

And a mixed bag

Philippa Pearce	Minnow on the Say	Oxford
	What the Neighbours Did and other stories	Kestrel
Eilis Dillon	The Cruise of the 'Santa Maria'	Faber
	The Island of Horses	
	The Lost Island	
Peter Dickinson	Emma Tupper's Diary	Gollancz
Noel Streatfeild	Ballet Shoes	Dent
	Curtain Up!	
	Thursday's Child	Collins
	The Growing Summer	

Three stories of escapes to the wild (with varied causes and results!)

'BB'	Brendon Chase	Benn
Jean George	My Side of the Mountain	Bodley Head
Joan G Robinson	Charley	Collins

and two stories by 'BB', for fishing enthusiasts:

'BB'	The Whopper	Benn
	The Pool of the Black Witch	Methuen

Five novels of the Second World War:

Ian Serraillier	The Silver Sword	Cape
Hester Burton	In Spite of All Terror	Oxford
Jill Paton Walsh	The Dolphin Crossing	Macmillan
Margaret Balderson	When Jays Fly to Barbmo	Oxford
Nina Bawden	Carrie's War	Gollancz

Two novels about physical handicap:

Ivan Southall	Let the Balloon Go	Methuen
Veronica Robinson	David in Silence	**Deutsch**

91

and one about mental handicap:

Roy Brown	*The River*	Abelard-Schuman

and the story of an autistic child:

Richard Parker	*He is Your Brother*	Brockhampton

and four particularly successful novels about working-class life:

John Rowe Townsend	*Widdershins Crescent*	Hutchinson
Sylvia Sherry	*A Pair of Jesus Boots*	Cape
Roy Brown	*Flight of Sparrows*	Abelard-Schuman
	White Sparrow	

Another mixed bag:

Philip Turner	*Colonel Sheperton's Clock*	Oxford
	The Grange at High Force	
	Sea Peril	
	War on the Darnel	

Modest and believable adventures; plenty of humour; but Philip Turner's particular achievement lies in presenting regular Christian observance as a natural and unembarrassing part of normal everyday living. In the secular climate of modern children's fiction this is quite an achievement.

Henri Bosco	*The Boy and the River*	Oxford
	The Fox in the Island	

Two distinguished novels by a gifted French writer. They go together, but in a relationship rather like that between *Tom Sawyer* and *Huckleberry Finn*—the second is much more demanding. Their distinctive atmosphere will be recognised by anyone who knows Alain Fournier's novel *Le Grand Meaulnes* ('The Lost Domain').

Sheena Porter	*Nordy Bank*	Oxford
	The Valley of Carreg-Wen	
Frederick Grice	*The Courage of Andy Robson*	
David Roth	*The Winds of Summer*	Abelard-Schuman
Henry Treece	*Ask for King Billy*	Faber

A secret service adventure, not to be confused with this author's historical novels. See also

Henry Treece	*Killer in Dark Glasses*	Faber
Emma Smith	*No Way of Telling*	Bodley Head
Margaret Storey	*Keep Running*	Faber
David Line	*Run For Your Life*	Cape

Some novels set in Australia and Tasmania:

Ivan Southall	*Ash Road*	Angus & Robertson
	Josh	
	The Fox Hole	Methuen
Mavis Thorpe Clark	*Wildfire*	Brockhampton Press
H F Brinsmead	*Isle of the Sea Horse*	Oxford
	Pastures of the Blue Crane	
	A Sapphire for September	Angus & Robertson

Hesba (H F) Brinsmead	Longtime Passing	
Nan Chauncy	They Found a Cave	
	World's End Was Home	
	High and Haunted Island	

and some set in the West Indies:

Andrew Salkey	Hurricane	Oxford
	Drought	
	Earthquake	
J Shirley Gudmundson	The Hurricane	World's Work
	The Turtle Net	
C Everard Palmer	My Father, Sun-Sun Johnson	Deutsch

Books by Arthur Ransome specially recommended:

Arthur Ransome	Swallows and Amazons	Cape
	We Didn't Mean to Go to Sea	
	Great Northern?	

Books by the French novelist, Paul Berna, specially recommended:

Paul Berna	Flood Warning	Bodley Head
	The Clue of the Black Cat	
	A Hundred Million Francs	

and a few others, strongly recommended too:

Allan Campbell McLean	The Hill of the Red Fox	Collins
Margaret Potter	The Touch-and-Go Year	Dennis Dobson
	The Blow-and-Grow Year	
Barbara Willard	The Family Tower	Kestrel
	The Toppling Towers	
	The Battle of Wednesday Week	
Ian Serraillier	They Raced for Treasure	Cape
Roy Brown	A Saturday in Pudney	Abelard-Schuman
	The Battle of Saint Street	
Dorothy Clewes	Storm Over Innish	Heinemann
Jenny Overton	Creed Country	Faber
	The Nightwatch Winter	
Ruth Tomalin	The Daffodil Bird	Faber
	The Spring House	
Catherine Storr	Rufus	
Jill Paton Walsh	Goldengrove	Macmillan
Jacynth Hope-Simpson	Save Tarranmoor!	Heinemann
Nicholas Fisk	High Way Home	Hamish Hamilton
Rodie Sudbery	A Curious Place	Deutsch
	Inside the Walls	

Two short, low-key, well-observed family stories, set respectively in Glasgow and York.

93

6 From Junior School to Secondary (2): Wider Horizons

The ordeal of facing up to new responsibilities and new feelings, sometimes prematurely, and of leaving childhood behind: this was the central topic of the last chapter, and in various guises it is the central preoccupation of readers in this age-group. But the experience may be set at a distance and explored less disturbingly in many other books for this age-group, particularly in what is loosely called 'historical fiction' and 'fantasy'. In this chapter I propose to look at some books of this kind and see what they too have to offer.

The 'historical novel' is not every child's taste, and despite its predominantly masculine themes it is most enjoyed by girls. Probably there are several reasons for this, but two at least are worth mentioning. Good historical novels are not easy to write, and authors who attempt them often take great trouble to research their backgrounds and provide accurate detail, especially in describing domestic life. Often, too, their emotional range is broader than a writer can freely introduce in modern settings, because it emerges from situations which are inherently tense and dramatic. These are topics which tend at this stage to involve girls deeply and make boys impatient. But once the first barriers are down (and one suspects that methods of teaching history are often sadly responsible for erecting them) there is a rich source of experience here for boys and girls alike.

The range of historical fiction is wide, and writers have choices to make. Three authors in particular—Cynthia Harnett, Rosemary Sutcliff and Leon Garfield—may help us to recognise the different kinds of appeal that historical fiction has to offer. All three have received the accolade of being awarded the Carnegie Medal (Cynthia Harnett for *The Woolpack*, Rosemary Sutcliff for *The Lantern Bearers* and Leon Garfield, jointly with Edward Blishen, for their retelling of classical myth in *The God Beneath the Sea*). All are scrupulous researchers and writers of distinctive skill, but there are striking differences in the product which emerges.

By far the most 'factual' of the three is Cynthia Harnett. This does not mean that her stories are more accurate in their detail than the others, only that her accuracy is more measured, systematic and blatant. A purist among history teachers could use her books as an adjunct to his teaching without being jabbed by his conscience. Her best books are set in the fifteenth century, and their weight and authenticity of domestic detail is such that any child, 'reading for the story', will scarcely escape uninformed. Her method can be readily seen in this passage from *The Writing on the Hearth*, in which the young and literate hero, Stephen, has been set to copy household documents:

'It was addressed to the Steward of Donnington Castle and it seemed to be just a long list of household stuff : "item : a glass jug and basin; a brass chafing dish; two leather pots" or "item : a bed of feathers with two pairs of blankets, a pair of sheets and hangings of striped serge," or "item : two turned chairs and four cushions". Clearly it was an inventory of things to be sent to Donnington when the family left Ewelme so that the Hall could be "sweetened". These periodical upheavals seemed to be a normal matter in great households. Stephen had often seen long lines of wagons and loaded baggage horses crossing Wallingford bridge, all belonging to some great lord who was leaving one of his houses, foul from occupation, to live for a while in another.'

The quality of this writing is clear : it has a hold on the realities of daily living, and is able to use particular details in a way which defines a wider social order. The plots of Cynthia Harnett's novels are all in keeping with this. In a way they are underplayed and unexciting, but one suspects that this is part of their purpose. Writing about a period of history which is usually associated with violent political upheaval, this author sets out to show the texture of ordinary living and the underlying economic forces which were largely undisturbed by dynastic conflicts.

We are left with books which are responsibly written, but perhaps a shade dull for the young reader who has not already acquired an appetite for history or realised that it is not all drums and trumpets. It is no insult to describe Cynthia Harnett's work as good teaching, in that she skilfully collects together a mass of illuminating detail which puts flesh and clothing on past societies, not fancy dress or empty masks. But this is *documentary historical fiction*, a valid kind of writing but not one which children are likely to enjoy until their taste-buds have been sharpened somewhere else.

Leon Garfield's work is the antithesis of Cynthia Harnett's. Her books show a painstaking quiescence and impersonality, and perhaps an over-rigorous self-denial. Garfield's have a stylish individualism which is atmospherically unique. This is not to say that no category fits them : they are *researched historical fantasy*—an honourable form which has attracted some distinguished writers. Garfield's settings—usually in the eighteenth century—are rendered with assured precision of detail quite comparable with Cynthia Harnett's, but the life they contain is shaped by a unique imagination. It is much too rich and complex to be summarised, but its characteristic tone is here in this short passage from the opening of *The Drummer Boy*. The scarlet-clad English army, marching up a hillside to the rhythm of its youthful drummer, has been ambushed and cut down :

'Where is the drummer boy now? Quite transfixed with terror and awe he marches on as grown men crash about him wearing crimson medals on their scarlet chests. His life seems charmed; and to many his fierce young face and shining drum are the last sight of all.

Now little suns seem to burst at the wood's edge—and violent thunderclaps shake the air. Flowers of smoke blossom among the regiments—and leave emptiness behind.

And still the regiments come on. Their courage is supernatural;

but their bodies are not. Some fifty yards from the hilltop there seems to be a toppling point that none can pass. Upright they come, then down they tumble, quite harvested.'

The paradox of Garfield's writing is that it *should* be intolerably morbid, but instead it is exuberant. Part of his imagination operates like a pathologist: it conducts autopsies on pieces of human wreckage, on broken bodies and severed limbs. It does so with an unwavering eye, a fierce unshrinking dispassionateness. In a way there is no other modern children's writer who presents mutilation and death more clinically than Garfield. Yet in a way there is no other who invests the darkness of human experience with more poetry, more dignity and bravery, or who transfixes it with a humour more deeply moral and compassionate. He peoples his world with human grotesques and explores the motivation of evil, most characteristically in a claustrophobic snare of fog or rain or darkness, yet out of it comes a bursting energy in his young heroes, and a resolute defiance of malignant fates, and a quite distinctive mingling of the heroic and the mock-heroic which can arouse simultaneous admiration and laughter. An episode in his first book, *Jack Holborn*, when the young hero flings away a fortune in jewels to purchase an enslaved friend, is an early example of the Garfield moment: the moment when absurdity and moral splendour are matchlessly combined.

Garfield's books are popular with children even though they make few concessions and are far from easy. They are very remarkable works, and in setting them against Cynthia Harnett's books we need to keep a distinction in mind: we are comparing two species of historical fiction, each offering an enjoyable experience when children are ready for it, and we are comparing deft, industrious craftsmanship with artistry. Garfield is one of several authors who make a nonsense of 'children's fiction' as a distinguishing term.

Rosemary Sutcliff perhaps lies between these two extremes. She also has a particular historical period which dominates her work: the closing phase of the Roman occupation in England

and the Dark Ages which followed. Like Garfield she has not kept strictly to this one historical preoccupation, and what is arguably her best novel, *Warrior Scarlet*, falls outside it. But the sense of a civilisation ending, and of encroaching barbarism, provides the kindling for her most characteristic work. These books too are researched and documented wherever possible, and dates, events and place-names are as authentic as they can be, but by its very nature, because it is largely undocumented and mysterious, this period offers free spaces for a writer's imagination. If Cynthia Harnett can be seen as a documentary historian in her novels, Rosemary Sutcliff is a creative historian in hers, and her authenticity depends on our belief in her sharp intuitive understanding of what it is like to be trapped in a disintegrating civilisation. She is at her best when she is dealing either with the highest ideals and demands a society has set for itself (as in *The Eagle of the Ninth*) or with the sharpest and most poignant sense of isolation at their loss (as in *Dawn Wind*). Her greatest achievement lies in her finesse in placing individuals against inexorable historical pressures.

It is the status of the individual in the work of these three writers which illustrates most clearly the difference between the kinds of historical fiction they write. Cynthia Harnett is in this way the most 'purely' historical: her characters are believable but not unduly interesting, and one can imagine them being interchanged with others without conspicuous effects on her work. Garfield's individuals are autonomous and dominant: his choice of setting provides the most striking backcloth for their egotisms. In Rosemary Sutcliff, concern for the individual, especially one kind of individual, not only supplies a further dimension in her work but explains it. Her central characters are depicted with great subtlety. They are independent of their circumstances in the sense that they are able to carry out important acts of will and choice, but they do not enjoy the independent selfhood of a Garfield figure. On the contrary, they are usually placed in situations where they have to struggle against both external and internal handicaps. They face not only a harsh environment but, more often than not, a severe personal disablement—mental or physical, but often physical. The distinctive feature of her work is that vividly rendered historical circumstances are enriched by this extra colouring of human endeavour. The brilliant *Warrior Scarlet*, set in prehistoric times, is an outstanding example. Its hero, Drem, belongs to a tribe which initiates its boys into manhood by demanding a ritual wolf-slaying. Boy and wolf meet in single combat: there is no aid, and no second chance. Failure brings demotion to the inferior shepherd-caste. For Drem this ordeal must be faced with the handicap of a withered arm, but no quarter is given him on that account. How Drem finally killed his wolf is the climax of a richly imagined novel: like so much of Rosemary Sutcliff's work, it could well be included with the books discussed in the next chapter, because she is so deeply concerned with difficulties to be surmounted and the winning of acceptance by the adult world. But her work also belongs here, because it is a most distinguished mode of historical fiction for the young. One word of warning: *Sword at Sunset* and *The Flowers of Adonis* are emphatically *not* children's books, and *The Mark of the Horse Lord* is so taxing that I have included it specifically as a book for older readers.

The historical novel has come a long way since the last war, and it would be quite unfair not to mention the writer chiefly responsible: Geoffrey Trease. *Bows Against the Barons*, his retold chronicle of Robin Hood which was first published in the 1930s, has recently been reissued and is still worth reading. It introduced a new social and political content into a rather tired genre, and set later writers free to discard old obligations. The balance of sympathies between Royalist and Roundhead in Rosemary Sutcliff's Civil War novel, *Simon*, would not have been possible without Trease's pioneering, and he is still producing strongly-plotted, well-researched novels like his recent story of the Italian Renaissance, *Horsemen on the Hills*.

This gives some idea of the strength and range of recent historical fiction. The days of romanticised gadzooksery seem happily over, and amongst the range of books available there is something for most readers—once the mystery of time has caught them.

For most children this particular imaginative nerve is first touched by time future rather than time past. Science fiction obviously has splendid potential for young readers, but the results to date have generally been disappointing: this is where we can expect the most exciting developments in the next few years. One opportunity at least, and a very important one, has not been missed. Imagine children of our own society, with feelings and values reflecting the generous disposition of a balanced and friendly youngster, transplanted into a world of alien beliefs and practices, more primitive and cruel and bigoted than our own (or perhaps not *more* so, but different enough to be seen for what they are). At once you have the basis of a story which is both exciting and thought-provoking. Of course this is not a new idea, but in the last few years it has taken on a new creative impetus. The facts of recent history partly account for it; our solid civilisation has turned paper-thin, and our social progress has ceased to seem irreversible. Man's nature has aroused daunting suspicions, and William Golding's *Lord of the Flies* is one product of them. Another is *The Chrysalids* by the late John Wyndham. Originally written as science fiction for adults, this is a book which I believe has exerted a powerful and benign effect on children's fiction.

Its best successor to date is almost certainly a magnificent trilogy of children's novels by Peter Dickinson: *The Weathermonger*, *Heartsease* and *The Devil's Children*. In these books Britain (only Britain, not even Ireland!) is suffering a period called 'The Changes', in which people have turned against all machines and reverted to primitive and brutal superstitions. A few children, unaffected by the 'Changes' or emerging from the spell, are trapped in a viciously intolerant society which will punish non-conformity with death. *The Weathermonger* relates the (hugely improbable) ending of the story, but the best of the three books is *Heartsease*, in which a group of children rescue a 'witch', actually an American spy, and convey him to safety in a renovated tugboat from the derelict wharves of Gloucester. *Heartsease* is a good example of the uncertainty which surrounds the judgement of children's literature. The book was discussed on the BBC programme 'A Choice of Paperbacks' on August 31st 1972. Basil Boothroyd, who chose it, commended it as 'escapist' reading, while another contributor, the politician David Steel, thought it 'a horrible book, in the sense of horror-provoking'. Both views strike me as most curious. One suspects that the 'escapist' tag is associated automatically with an adventure story for children, and caused Mr Boothroyd to overlook the book's overriding concern for humane behaviour and for resolute courage in the cause of civilised principle—not the kind of concern which is glaringly evident in much 'realistic' fiction for adults. As for Mr Steel, his squeamishness does credit to his concern for children, but not to his knowledge of them. It is one purpose of this book to propose some demarcation lines, beyond which lies the kind of writing to which children should not be exposed, but *Heartsease* lies so far within those lines as not to raise a qualm. It does contain some violence, but nothing that is likely to cause the slightest distress to a child of normal resilience. I cannot imagine that *Heartsease,* or the other books in Peter Dickinson's trilogy, could fail to give most young readers the pleasure of an exciting story underpinned by a set of manifestly sane and desirable social values. But since the book clearly arouses conflicting opinions, it is one of several discussed in this book which parents would find it interesting (and, I hope, enjoyable) to read for themselves.

Another able writer of such 'futurist' fiction is John Christopher, whose trilogy of books on a similar theme to Peter Dickinson's—and even more clearly in line of descent from *The Chrysalids*—began in 1970 with *The Prince in Waiting.*

When one puts together books like these it becomes clear that what are broadly termed 'historical novels', 'science fiction' and 'fantasies' offer much the same kind of imaginative experience, and there is a quite mistaken tendency to regard 'historical novels' as somehow being more worthwhile. In short, reading a 'historical novel' is not a valuable enterprise for a child because he learns some history from it; it is valuable because it cultivates his sense of variety and difference in human life, and brings together the homely and the strange. Quite literally, in the old trite phrase, it widens his horizons. This is exhilarating, or should be: it is the enchantment of the golden bird in Yeats' poem, who sang

> '. . . to lords and ladies of Byzantium
> Of what is past, or passing, or to come.'

After all, the two dimensions on which everyone is forced to build his conception of the world are those of time and space, and the books which sharpen our awareness of them are doing us a service. Books like Peter Dickinson's transfer recognisable children into unrecognisable future times. Others explore the dimension of time itself, opening the closed doors of history and transmitting children into periods other than their own. For what may seem like a small cul-de-sac of children's literature this one is remarkably well-populated.

Sometimes the door opens into the future (as in David Severn's *The Future Took Us*); sometimes it opens into the past, as in Joan G Robinson's *When Marnie Was There*. In this story, set on the East Anglian coast, a young, isolated, friendless girl, dispatched to the seaside for mental recuperation, forms a friendship with another girl, mysterious and strangely-dressed, who lives in a large house by the waterside. It is only belatedly that she realises where 'Marnie' lives—in time past—and later still when she finds who Marnie was, but by that time she has formed the gift of friendship and is set free in the companionships of her own age. Although this story is perhaps too easily idyllic (time fantasies of this kind are inescapably saddening, and the sadness inherent in this story is too briskly dismissed) it does express a truth about loneliness and friendship which lifts it above the average novel. It is very much a book for girls.

Lucy M Boston's brilliant 'Green Knowe' books are also time fantasies of this kind, and are easily understandable for quite young children. Yet Mrs Boston has recently disclosed that it was only her insistence on illustrations—exquisitely drawn by her son—which caused the first 'Green Knowe' novel to be published as a children's book at all. They do not belong exclusively to juniors, any more than Alison Uttley's *A Traveller in*

Time is exclusively for adults, though it could readily be classified as an adult novel: as usual the categories are inadequate.

A Traveller in Time is one of the best of all time fantasies. It is set in the Derbyshire background which Mrs Uttley renders so well in her autobiography *The Country Child*, and transports a sensitive youngster to and fro between modern times and the Elizabethan age. That long-ago world is one of high political intrigue, and the book centres on the Babington plot to free Mary Queen of Scots from her imprisonment at Wingfield Manor. The outcome of such plottings is a matter of historical fact, and the book does not shirk the tragedy inherent in its picture of doomed hope and futile adventure. Yet counterpoised against this is the rich vitality of its domestic setting, and its marvellous concrete depiction of Elizabethan home-life—a life of daily routine and periodic festival as well as political machination. *A Traveller in Time* is an excellent example of the experience which time-fantasy is specially equipped to give —a more than usually acute sense of wonderment at the realities of historical change and continuity, because the experience is directly shared with a participant in the story. As we read, our imagination receives a series of vivid promptings from a character whose identity can merge with our own. Because of this, these stories are perhaps the best of all in helping a child reader to apprehend the mystery of time.

By common consent among critics of children's literature this kind of story has produced in recent years at least one unmistakable classic of children's fiction: Philippa Pearce's *Tom's Midnight Garden*. The basic situation of the story is fairly familiar, and illuminating by its frequency. Many of these stories concern a solitary child—solitary either by temperament or circumstance—and often one who is either ill or likely to be; the child is uprooted from home and left in new surroundings. In these settings of suspenseful isolation the strange happenings begin. Although this may simply be a convenient plot-device and nothing more, the imaginative distinction of many such stories does suggest that authors have found here a situation of absorbing interest—a situation, that is, where a child is peculiarly open to new experiences which may mark his character indelibly. Quite often the new surroundings have a kind of antique warmth about them which is both inviting and quaint—they are historically obsolete themselves, before anything happens to reveal a still remoter world.

Tom's Midnight Garden, on the other hand, begins in a setting which is bleakly up-to-date. True, Tom is undergoing compulsory solitude (he is in quarantine for measles), but there is nothing romantic about his prison-house. He is dispatched to a childless aunt and uncle, who occupy a flat in a converted Victorian house. The apartment is reasonably sized for these days—that is to say, small. His uncle's mind is also indefatigably reasonable—that is to say, small. Tom in his solitude is over-burdened with the sensible; and sensible rules for boys of his age dictate that ten hours each night should be spent in bed. But something at least is not sensible—the old grandfather clock in the hall, which belongs to the house's cantankerous owner, Mrs Bartholomew. The grandfather clock does something which sensible clocks eschew: it strikes thirteen. At dead of night, when the clock strikes the time-which-is-not, Tom escapes from his captivity in the flat and finds behind the house the garden of the house as it was long ago, and here Tom finds a friend. For one hour a night, an hour which the mad grandfather clock takes out of time, he is free in the garden with Hatty, a girl from a time now lost.

The garden, though, is not timeless, and years pass by there in the space of Tom's brief midnight visits. Tom grows older by a few days, Hatty by much longer; she grows up. Who she is, and how the story is at last most perfectly resolved, are all part of a beautifully shaped and rounded novel in which every detail and every small event have their significance.

Of course few young readers will be consciously aware of the book's narrative finesse. At the beginning of the story, sensible, reasonable Uncle Alan refuses to let Tom climb the tower of Ely Cathedral (he is, after all, in quarantine), so Tom is given a photograph of the cathedral instead. At the end, that postcard has its part in one of the two great moments in the story—when, at the summit of Ely Cathedral, the present enters fully into the past; at the second great moment it is the past which enters fully into the present. This careful blending of detail and significance is one of the qualities which make *Tom's Midnight Garden* a great children's book. It is easy to say that writing of this kind is over-subtle and that children will never catch the point of it. Consciously, probably not. Nor does an adult theatre audience 'catch' the complete verbal rhythms of a Shakespeare play. This conscious level is not the one at which we usually listen or read, and we can sense a cohesion and unity, and get pleasure from them, without being able to explain how they occur. The pleasure which children find in *Tom's Midnight Garden* is partly a response to controlled verbal artistry. It is not the kind of pleasure they can always enjoy, any more than adults could attend continuously to *King Lear*; we are looking here at works which, in their very different fields, achieve extreme excellence. We can say, as I have already said, that children, like adults, do not always need such excellence; but it is not wasted.

So far in this chapter we have ranged from realistic historical fiction through to a kind of fantasy in which past and future meet. To complete the picture we should look at one more writer of considerable distinction who takes this process a stage further. This is Joan Aiken, the author of a remarkable series of interconnected books beginning with *The Wolves of Willoughby Chase*. In Joan Aiken's work, history is not simply raided: it is inverted, turned topsy-turvy with a rash abandon that few writers would care to risk. The ostensible period of her books is the early nineteenth century, but it is not a period that any historian would recognise. The English throne is occupied by the House of Stuart, but it is constantly threatened by Hanoverian plottings and insurrections. It is a world of fast-moving horse-drawn coaches and snail-paced trains, of Dickensian industrial cities and wolf-infested wilderness, a world which (in *Night Birds on Nantucket*) combines a navy under sail with a form of ballistic missile capable of shooting accurately across the width of the Atlantic.

The Wolves of Willoughby Chase by Joan Aiken,
illustrated by Pat Marriott

One could easily be suspicious of these books. The trouble is that they have such obvious appeal for a widely-read adult. After all, these outrageous games at the expense of history are only funny if one knows the truth of it, and they are only the beginning. The hideous criminal governess, Letitia Slighcarp, who figures in both *The Wolves of Willoughby Chase* and *Night Birds on Nantucket*, is more enjoyably horrific if one has encountered such characters as Miss Murdstone in *David Copperfield*. Captain Casket, the whaling skipper, who drives his ship round mighty seas in obsessive pursuit of a pink whale, has richer comic associations if one's mind is already coloured by *Moby Dick*.

Moreover, this kind of appeal to adult literary sophistication is compounded by a mass of linguistic jokes, often turning on people's names : who but Miss Aiken would dream of christening a German gunnery expert Axeltree Breadno? Or, in somewhat more sinister fashion, give a (rather kindly) doctor the surname Mayhew?

In short, these books are verbally rich, full of sophisticated linguistic comedy. But the book which appeals so obviously to adults is not automatically well written for children, and there are several well-known authors who arouse adults to enthusiasm which children do not share. It would be fair to say of Joan Aiken that she will only be enjoyed by children who have begun to appreciate the variety and comic potential of language, but once that taste has been acquired she is a writer who can give tremendous pleasure. Her language, like her history, obeys no rules—the absurdities of both are limitless, and there is something for everybody.

To see her work as simply historical comedy is not enough, however. She is a truly comic writer—in short, her stories are not just absurd adventures, but are in their own way extremely serious, as all true comedy is. In the two books I have mentioned so far the emphasis is certainly on hilarious escapades, and the same is true of the splendid extravaganza which comes between them, *Black Hearts in Battersea*. Yet even in these early books there is a raw nerve of pain, as the books touch on the tensions of love and loyalty, the perils of delicacy and weakness, the sufferings of old age, the harsh longings of homesickness. This strain of emotional realism is there from the first, but it makes itself most firmly felt with the advent of Miss Aiken's incomparable girl heroine, Dido Twite, who first appears in *Black Hearts in Battersea.*

Of all the child heroes and heroines of modern children's fiction, Dido Twite is the one for whom I would most confidently predict immortality. She appears in several books, and indeed all Miss Aiken's novels intersect and overlap in complicated ways, forming an intricate composite pattern. This is one reason why her books are best read in order of composition, but another and more important reason is the steady deepening of emotional strength and complexity from book to book. Some emotional harshness is not spared us in these first three books, but in the fourth, *The Whispering Mountain,* Joan Aiken's work reaches a new level of intensity. This book ends with the death of Tom Dando, the poet-father of a principal child-character. In the last chapter I objected to a particular way of presenting the death of parents, but I do not suggest that the topic is inherently improper, and this episode in *The Whispering Mountain* shows how admirably it can be handled. The book is a fantasy, but it is peopled by real, keenly-drawn people with real emotions; its events are exciting, funny, and sad; it affirms the value of life with great energy and vitality, and in the life and work of Tom Dando that value is affirmed with bell-like clarity. So it is in his death, and the manner of it. In the context of the story, death becomes an acceptable part of the experience of living, not without pain, not beyond bearing.

The last chapter began with *Tom Sawyer,* and its interplay of reality and dream. The other books discussed in these two chapters cover many modes from unrelenting realism to the outermost reaches of fantasy—or, as some readers would contend, mere whimsical self-indulgence. I do not share this last view, because in all these books—so good of their kind and so varied in nature—I see concerns and qualities in common, above all a concern to give children the kind of experience that makes for growing. At one extreme we have a realism which may demand too much; at the other there is no 'escapism' though there is plenty of escape, and should be. Taken together these very varied books offer a composite experience which touches on many important themes, and in the book-list there are chances to explore these further.

The age-group we have had in mind in these two chapters is the most unpredictable and unclassifiable of all. So is its literature. Some of the books discussed here will be enjoyed by younger children, and others may well be left to a later stage. This has to be the longest and the central section of the book because it has no precise boundaries at either end—the experiences it covers are central and erratic, explosive and prolonged. The books I have chosen should form an enjoyable part of it, but we should be ready for anything. Just what that 'anything' might be is amusingly caught by Michael Innes, in a reading-list compiled by the youthful hero of his novel, *The Journeying Boy*, and I leave it to speak for itself:

'Please deliver at once by special messenger one pair of binoculars for bird-watching and a good camera (not box). Please send also these books: *Biggles Flies East, Biggles Flies West, Biggles Flies North, Biggles Fails to Return*, Bertrand Russell's *History of Western Philosophy*, George Moore's *Daphnis and Chloe, Biggles and the Camel Squadron*, Bleinstein's *More and More Practical Sex*, Blunden's *Life of Shelley*, also *Atalanta in Calydon, Biggles in Borneo, Women in Love*, and any *close* translations of Caesar's *Civil Wars*.'

BOOK-LIST FOR JUNIOR SCHOOL TO SECONDARY (2)
(See the note on pp. 37–39)

In this list are some books which draw the imagination into other worlds, past or future, once-real, never-real, or maybe-one-day. Historical fiction, for which many children profess dislike, takes many different forms, some of which are discussed in this chapter. The list of historical novels is intentionally *not* sub-divided in this way, because it is a good idea to experiment, and the reader in any case reacts more often to the individual author than to the type of story.

Some historical novels:

Rhoda Power	*Redcap Runs Away*	Cape

The Middle Ages; but a choice between home and wandering which many people still have to make.

Morna Stewart	*Marassa and Midnight*	Heinemann
Elizabeth Borton de Trevino	*I, Juan de Pareja*	Gollancz

Two stories based on the theme of slavery.

Geoffrey Trease	*The Crown of Violet*	Macmillan
	The Hills of Varna	

Two fine stories offering a rich sense of historical connection. The first recounts the story of a Greek comedy, and how it came to be composed, the second concerns the rediscovery of the play many centuries later. See also many other titles, including

	Bows Against the Barons	Brockhampton

An early book by Geoffrey Trease to which later writers owe much. Not to be confused with him is

Henry Treece	*The Children's Crusade*	Bodley Head
	Viking's Dawn	
	Horned Helmet	Brockhampton

Treece's best work concerns the period of the Vikings. Mollie Hunter, whose folk-lore tales have been discussed earlier, writes excellent historical novels for older readers, including:

Mollie Hunter	*The Lothian Run*	Hamish Hamilton
	The Spanish Letters	Evans
	Hi Johnny	
	The Stronghold	Hamish Hamilton

Some stories of ancient history:

Hans Baumann	*I Marched with Hannibal*	Oxford
J G Fyson	*The Three Brothers of Ur*	
and its sequel	*The Journey of the Eldest Son*	
Elizabeth George Speare	*The Bronze Bow*	Gollancz

The story of guerilla struggles against the Romans in the time of Jesus.

Rosemary Sutcliff	*Warrior Scarlet*	Oxford

Perhaps the best of all Rosemary Sutcliff's novels, set in prehistoric Britain.

The following novels by Rosemary Sutcliff are set in the last phase of the Roman occupation, and the English Dark Ages. They are suitable mainly for children of twelve and over, and are appropriate for adolescent readers:

Rosemary Sutcliff	*The Eagle of the Ninth*	Oxford
	Outcast	
	The Silver Branch	
	The Lantern Bearers	
	Dawn Wind	
	The Shield Ring	

Also for readers interested in the Dark Ages and the Norman Conquest:

Kevin Crossley-Holland and Jill Paton Walsh	*Wordhoard*	Macmillan

A brilliant collection of stories, including one about Alfred which may lead on to

C Walter Hodges	*The Namesake*	Bell
	The Marsh King	

and one about Harold which may lead on to

Hilda Lewis	*Harold Was My King*	Oxford
Howard Jones	*Falconsdale*	Blackie

For readers interested in the Middle Ages:

Cynthia Harnett	*The Wool-Pack*	Methuen
	The Load of Unicorn	
	The Writing on the Hearth	
Rosemary Sutcliff	*Knight's Fee*	Oxford
Rosemary Weir	*High Courage*	Faber
Jill Paton Walsh	*The Emperor's Winding Sheet*	Macmillan

Amongst several good novels dealing partly with the Elizabethan theatre are:

Geoffrey Trease	*Cue for Treason*	Blackwell
Antonia Forest	*The Player's Boy*	Faber
	The Player and the Rebels	

The following are some books from Ronald Welch's history of the Carey family, extending in time from the reign of Elizabeth I to the First World War:

Ronald Welch	*The Hawk*	Oxford
	For the King	
	Captain of Dragoons	
	Mohawk Valley	
	Nicholas Carey	
	Tank Commander	

An admirable family-based chronicle history.

Another family chronicle, set in sixteenth- and seventeenth-century Sussex:

Barbara Willard	*The Lark and the Laurel*	Kestrel
	The Sprig of Bloom	
	A Cold Wind Blowing	
	The Iron Lily	
	Harrow and Harvest	

The novels of Leon Garfield, mainly set in the eighteenth century:

Leon Garfield	*Jack Holborn*	Kestrel
	Smith	
	Black Jack	
	Devil-in-the-Fog	
	The Drummer Boy	

Post-industrial times, the nineteenth-century origins of our own day:

Hester Burton	*No Beat of Drum*	Oxford
K M Peyton	*Windfall*	
Walter Unsworth	*The Devil's Mill*	Gollancz
	Whistling Clough	
Marjorie Darke	*Ride the Iron Horse*	Kestrel
	The Star Trap	
Catherine Cookson	*Our John Willie*	Macdonald
Philip Turner	*Steam on the Line*	Oxford
and its sequel	*Devil's Nob*	Hamish Hamilton
Gillian Avery	*A Likely Lad*	Collins

Some time-fantasies:

Philippa Pearce	*Tom's Midnight Garden*	Oxford
Alison Uttley	*A Traveller in Time*	Faber
Lucy M Boston	*The Children of Green Knowe*	

and see also the rest of the excellent 'Green Knowe' series.

Penelope Lively	*The Driftway*	Heinemann
Joan G Robinson	*When Marnie Was There*	Collins
Penelope Farmer	*Charlotte Sometimes*	Evans
	Emma in Winter	
Jane Louise Curry	*The Daybreakers*	Kestrel
	Over the Sea's Edge	
Richard Parker	*The Old Powder Line*	Gollancz
Glyn Frewer	*Adventure in Forgotten Valley*	Faber
Ronald Welch	*The Gauntlet*	Oxford
Madeleine l'Engle	*A Wrinkle in Time*	Kestrel
John Masefield	*The Box of Delights*	Heinemann
Dennis Hamley	*Pageants of Despair*	Deutsch
David Severn	*The Girl in the Grove*	Allen & Unwin
Pamela Sykes	*Come Back, Lucy*	Hamish Hamilton
Meta Mayne Reid	*The Glen Beyond the Door*	Faber

The last, an older book written before the present troubles, gives a remarkable insight into the origins of tragedy in Northern Ireland.

The historical fantasies of Joan Aiken:

Joan Aiken	*The Wolves of Willoughby Chase*	Cape
	Black Hearts in Battersea	
	Night Birds on Nantucket	
	The Whispering Mountain	
	The Cuckoo Tree	

Some fantasies:

J R R Tolkien	*The Hobbit*	Allen & Unwin
Penelope Lively	*The Wild Hunt of Hagworthy*	Heinemann
	The Whispering Knights	
	Astercote	
	The Ghost of Thomas Kempe	
	The House in Norham Gardens	
Catherine Storr	*Marianne Dreams*	Faber
Mary Q Steele	*The First of the Penguins*	Macmillan
Alan Garner	*The Weirdstone of Brisingamen*	Collins
	The Moon of Gomrath	
	Elidor	

The first two books have perhaps been overpraised, but the third, arguably Garner's best novel to date, is beautifully done.

Susan Cooper	*Over Sea, Under Stone*	Chatto and Windus
	The Dark is Rising	
	Greenwitch	
Jane Louise Curry	*Beneath the Hill*	Dobson
	The Sleepers	

There is a considerable overlap of interest in the above books in this section; readers who enjoy any of them are likely to enjoy them all.

Leon Garfield	*The Ghost Downstairs*	Kestrel
Elizabeth Goudge	*The Little White Horse*	Brockhampton
Robert Druce	*Firefang*	Bell
Josephine Poole	*Billy Buck*	Hutchinson
Nicholas Fisk	*Grinny*	Heinemann
Clive King	*The Town That Went South*	Hamish Hamilton
Richard Church	*The French Lieutenant*	Heinemann
Nicholas Stuart Gray	*Mainly in Moonlight*	Faber
John Gordon	*The Giant Under the Snow*	Hutchinson
Russell Hoban	*The Mouse and His Child*	Faber

This is another unclassifiable book. Based on the wanderings and ultimate homecoming of a damaged clockwork toy, it is also a novel of deep insight and compassion, which can be read at many levels of meaning.

The following trilogy, which can also be read at many levels, is included elsewhere under the list of 'Adolescent Reading', but it will also be enjoyed by many younger readers; it is, without much doubt, a new classic of children's fiction.

Ursula le Guin	*A Wizard of Earthsea*	Gollancz
	The Tombs of Atuan	
	The Farthest Shore	

Two trilogies, each concerned with a future England which has reverted to earlier and more primitive ways of life:

Peter Dickinson	*The Weathermonger*	Gollancz
	Heartsease	
	The Devil's Children	
John Christopher	*The Prince in Waiting*	Hamish Hamilton
	Beyond the Burning Lands	
	The Sword of the Spirits	

and the book, originally intended for adults, which awakened much interest in this theme:

| John Wyndham | *The Chrysalids* | Michael Joseph |

Some science fiction:

James Blish	*The Star-Dwellers*	Faber
	Welcome to Mars	
Arthur C Clarke	*Of Time and Stars*	Gollancz
	Dolphin Island	
Alan E Nourse	*Star Surgeon*	Faber
	Scavengers in Space	
Hugh Walters	*Operation Columbus*	
	Destination Mars	
Andre Norton	*Moon of Three Rings*	Kestrel
	Exiles of the Stars	
	Lord of Thunder	Gollancz
	Sargasso of Space	

7 What Place for the Classics?

If there is one place above all where adult attitudes towards children's reading are sharply polarised, it is in front of the classics shelf. Some parents and teachers firmly believe that children should be provided with nothing but the best, and be progressively introduced to the rich literature they have inherited. Others, with recollections of prize-days and unwanted presents, of austere binding, gilt lettering, and a formidable wad of closely-printed pages, insist that premature exposure to classic literature can only spoil, perhaps for ever, the pleasure that children might later discover for themselves.

As always, there is some truth on both sides. In a book about children's fiction it seems only fair to seek help with the answer from a fictional child. Here, cooped up to his great annoyance on a rainy day, is Paddy Weir, the young hero of Ruth Tomalin's story, *The Sea Mice*. Paddy is rummaging in the attic:

'He found a book called *Tom Brown's Schooldays*. The leaves were yellow with age, brown-speckled, and with an odd pleasant smell, like boiling rice. On the fly-leaf was written "To Patrick Weir, on his 9th birthday, from Mother. Herons, Dundee, April 3rd, 1900."

A strange thought struck Paddy. He began to count on his fingers, and it dawned on him that this "Patrick Weir" was not his father but his grandfather. A grandfather nine years old! Paddy laughed and opened the book. There were pictures of boys in short jackets, white collars, top hats, long trousers: playing football, fighting, running across muddy fields. He yawned, and was just going to toss it on to the pile of rubbish, when another picture caught his eye. It showed a boy dancing in horror, with a

115

snake twined round his leg, and a rat peering out of his trouser-pocket. . . .

Paddy forgot his temper. He forgot the rain outside . . . He sat down, planted himself against an old trunk and turned back to the beginning of the story.'

Paddy skips the first three chapters, but is soon caught up in the account of Tom's first, cold journey to Rugby.

'Paddy's toes felt numb with frost as he read, until the guard muffled his feet in straw. He heard the jingling harness, the ring of the horses' hooves on the road, the guard's horn; he saw the lamps shining through the fog; he smelt the steaming horses and the "shag" smoked by passing workmen.'

The Sea Mice is not only a sensitive and original story for younger children; it is also a delicate, convincing account of the way children respond to the stories they read and hear. Paddy, who is about eight years old at this time, stumbles on an uninviting book when his own mood is sullen and unreceptive. A chance detail catches his attention, he skips and tests a chapter or two, and then is drawn into rapt involvement in the story. Later on, when he himself is going to school and passes through St Albans in the cold, his recollection of this story dispels his gloom.

What might it pay us to notice in all this? First of all, Paddy chooses the book for himself: no one gives it to him as 'suitable' reading. In some ways it is clearly unsuitable for an eight-year-old, and Paddy's understanding is strictly limited. He takes from it what he can understand and enjoy, guesses at some meanings, and skips the rest. Secondly, the whole event depends on pure chance—he glimpses arresting detail which detains his attention. Once this has happened, all other unpropitious circumstances, including the condition of the book, fade to insignificance. Thirdly, once he is under way his attention is total and complete, surviving all linguistic obstacles. Lastly, the chance imaginative experience of a rainy afternoon remains with him as a source of future strength and reassurance.

The most important thing to notice is the haphazardness of the whole proceeding. When we are dealing with modern stories (and these probably include some future classics) we are on firmer ground : we may know that a child has previously liked a particular author, or that the subject is one in which the child is already interested, and we can guess with some confidence that a book is 'too young' or 'too old'. The less distinguished the material, the more right we are likely to be.

When we come to the classics, however, most people with experience of children's reading will know how few rules apply. One child may spurn an attractive edition of *Treasure Island* which ought to be a sure success; another may be found reading *Pride and Prejudice* with the same involvement that we saw in Paddy Weir. A famous children's book like *Little Women* or *The Wind in the Willows* may be read with delight ten years or more after it was first given, and the adult enjoy what the child rejected, but taxing masterpieces never intended for children, such as *Jane Eyre* or *Wuthering Heights*, may be read with enormous pleasure by eleven-year-olds.

I take it as a golden rule, then, that if you wish to choose a classic novel as a gift for any child or young adult, you should not be surprised or disappointed or feel that the gift is a failure, if its recipient merely gives it a passing glance, and lays it aside. Its time may come many years later, or it may soon cohere with a passing mood, or connect with a pressing interest, and suddenly become meaningful, as *Tom Brown's Schooldays* did for Paddy. The very least that can happen is that you will have added another potentially important experience to those that are lying around, waiting for their moment. The more of them, the better : lying around waiting is a praiseworthy activity for books.

If the gift of a classic is looked at in this way—more as a premium bond than a pound note—it is as well to make sure that the gift is desirable. The case for buying paperbacks rather than hard-bound books is less strong in the case of works which may have to wait a long time for their turn, and hardback classics are usually cheaper than modern works because they are produced in greater quantities and there are no royalties to pay.

Unfortunately it is still true that many standard series are very uninviting—they have dull and uniform jackets and bindings, diaphanous paper and overcrowded print, and the illustrations, if they exist, are usually poor. These series should be avoided: the appearance of a book is very important to all young readers, and it is much wiser to settle for an attractive edition, with a colourful binding which will, after all, long outlive the dust cover, even if it means greater expense. Details of attractive editions published specially for children are included in the book-list.

Another decision which buyers have to make in selecting classics is whether to settle for anything less than the full unaltered text, which may be daunting in length and complexity. The market's presentation of a classic work can range from the zany scholarship of *The Annotated Alice* (ed. Martin Gardner) to strip-cartoon versions reminiscent of the picture-strip *Macbeth*, in which Lady Macbeth is seen flourishing a bloodstained knife and announcing 'I fixed it!' In most cases, however, the available compromise is likely to be an abridged or rewritten version of the story.

Purists will accept neither, believing that a diluted classic is a lost classic. At the other extreme are those who believe that children read only for a story, not for a style, and that since the great classics are usually splendid tales, it is absurd to impose needless linguistic obstacles. As usual, the truth seems to lie between the two extremes.

Parents even of very small children soon begin to find that a sense of patterned language as something to be enjoyed is an early characteristic of language acquisition. Stylistic effects with specific names—rhyme, alliteration, assonance, metre, periodic repetition—are the very stuff of nursery rhymes and infant language games. Refrains and repetitions, and all manner of devices for making language organised and predictable, are crucial to verbal enjoyment and a sense of linguistic possibilities. Increasingly, too, children become aware of the weaponry of organised language in deflation and ridicule. (For a magnificent collection of such language, see *The Lore and Language of*

Schoolchildren by Iona and Peter Opie.) A willingness to explore and enjoy language in this way is something to be cherished, and the stylistic uniqueness of a great writer may well stimulate it. In this respect at least the purists are correct : a sense of style in language is both more readily acquired, and more readily lost, than we suppose.

But we can hardly insist that great language should never be tampered with. Strictly interpreted, this would mean that no classic should ever be translated, or filmed, or televised, or even illustrated. Scarcely anyone would question the right of good scriptwriters and directors to interpret a writer's work for the screen, and it is a commonplace that indifferent books sometimes make great films. We judge by the results, and we need to do the same in problems of adaptation or abridgement.

Some potentially enjoyable books are too forbiddingly long to be fitted into the experience-crowded life of a modern child, but skilful abridgement can bring these within range. Some books contain scenes or episodes which, for moral or psychological reasons, we would not wish a young child to read, and these can often be omitted without damage to the story. (But it needs to be said again that censorship of this kind is a hit-and-miss affair : at the individual level it is almost impossible to predict what will distress a particular child, and at the more general level we need to remember that children are frequently less squeamish than adults.) Some classics not intended for children, but widely read by them are sometimes gripping and sometimes tedious. *Gulliver's Travels* is a clear example : of the many children who enjoy the Lilliputian episode, few are interested in Laputa. Excessive length, or serious linguistic difficulty, or near-certain distress or tedium, can all justify the practice of careful abridgement. But all publishers should make it clear when a book has been abridged (at present many do not) and name the abridger, as someone exercising a reputable craft (at present almost no publishers do this, though radio and television do so as a matter of course).

The book which is not simply abridged but re-written is a greater problem. To begin with, there has to be a clear distinction between the re-written version of a classic novel by a known author, and the re-written version of an ancient story which may already have been re-told many times. The first of these things is literature reconditioned, the second is literature re-made. A simplified version of *Great Expectations* may have the virtue of opening up a good story for children who would otherwise miss it, but the prospect of its improving on the original is remote. But the ancient classic stories of history and myth have no one's monogram on them. They belong to everyone, and belong to every generation in a new way. The Arthurian legend is changed and renewed from century to century in the work of the Gawain Poet, of Malory, and of Tennyson, and in our own time was further transformed by T H White in *The Once and Future King*: for each writer the general myth is transformed into something distinctively his own. In particular the figure of Merlin continues to prompt the English imagination and make unexpected appearances, as he does for instance in Peter Dickinson's excellent story *The Weathermonger*. In such re-working of old myths there is no theft, and no inevitable weakening of the story: on the contrary, it may take on new and rich associations.

For children this kind of re-writing, the re-telling and re-working of myth, is not just acceptable but very important. At every stage of education from infancy to adolescence, one hears from teachers who care about such things that the traditional inheritance of story can no longer be taken for granted. Nursery rhymes and traditional fairy tales are not known to many small children, and at a later stage they appear to by-pass the native Arthurian legend, the classic myths of Greece and Rome, the great stories of the Nordic sagas, and those of the Bible itself. Whether teachers are right in sensing a decline in such things is questionable, of course. Classical legend can never have been really familiar to more than a minority of children, and the Norse legends to fewer still: today there is probably a higher proportion than ever before who have come across them at some time. But the other tendencies probably do exist. Nursery rhymes are tending to be less the communal property of childhood, and more the deliberate concern of literate and conscientious parents, while the slackening hold on biblical story is a readily observable event, with causes which are not my concern here.

Where such a decline exists, there are many reasons for regretting it. For the purposes of this book the main one is that these are *good* stories. The story of Humpty Dumpty, the story of Cinderella, the story of Sir Lancelot, the story of Ulysses, the story of Njal, the story of David, the story of Christ : all of them, for the stage at which we come to know them, are more than stories, of course. Anecdote, fable, legend or truth, they have survived because they have helped many generations to get their bearings, to draw a personal map of the world, marked with the scenes of fundamental disaster and triumph. But whatever else they are, whether a tale for an evening or a geography of spiritual understanding, they are stories first and foremost, and their initial narrative hold on the listening imagination is crucial to their effect. They need to be continually re-made by new storytellers as well as re-heard from the old ones, and acquire the resonances of each new age. Our children need to hear them or read them in a form they can enjoy.

There are, then, two forms of the re-told classic story which can be recommended unreservedly for young readers. One is the straight, clear, unadorned retelling of the classic tale itself, where the modern writer tries to interfere as little as possible with the anonymity of the original story. This kind of book includes translations of stories in 'dead' or irretrievable languages like Latin, classical Greek, and Anglo-Saxon, and distinguished work of this sort has been done by such writers as Roger Lancelyn Green, Ian Serraillier, Rosemary Sutcliff and Kevin Crossley-Holland. The other kind of retelling is the strongly individual exploration of a traditional theme, departing freely from the lines of the inherited story at the prompting of the writer's own imagination, and making of it something fresh and original. In my view, one of the finest modern examples of such storytelling is Rosemary Harris's biblical trilogy beginning with *The Moon in the Cloud*. It is useful to keep these two categories distinct, and in the book-list for this chapter I have included some examples of each. There are no dependable guidelines to suggest a measure of suitability for particular age-groups, but roughly speaking the 'anonymous' story is appreciated more by younger children, and the original versions by older readers.

In the case of traditional stories, re-telling is an important and welcome practice. The other kind of 'classic', when the author is known to us and his style and narrative methods unique, the business of re-writing is much more dubious. In a great modern novel the tale is inseparable from the manner of its telling, and it is usually wiser to settle for the original, abridged where necessary, than for some kind of 'digest' (which is usually so speedily digestible that it can't be tasted on the way down).

We have already noticed, in passing, another distinction we need to make clear : the difference between the 'classic' story which was always intended for children (*Coral Island*, *Treasure Island*, *The Swiss Family Robinson*, *Bevis*, *Alice in Wonderland*, *Tom Brown's Schooldays*, *Little Women*) and the one which was written for adults but which many children read (*Jane Eyre*, *Wuthering Heights*, *Gulliver's Travels*, and so on). The difference is complicated by an awkward fact : some books, such as *Robinson Crusoe* and *Gulliver's Travels*, have been so firmly appropriated by young readers that they have almost become pure 'children's' classics by accident; others, such as *Alice in Wonderland* and *The Wind in the Willows*, often give greater pleasure to adults than to children and can be read prematurely.

Once again this indicates that it is unrealistic to make sharp distinction between the 'children's book' and any other kind of book : it is as true of the classics as anywhere else, and perhaps more so. Great books are composed from a complex of interests and motives, and are understandable at a number of different levels. If we look more closely for a moment at a few of these splendid, highly inconvenient books, we can perhaps discover some reasons for their unstable, multiple appeal.

Alice in Wonderland, of all books, is the most conspicuous example of a children's classic thieved by adults. Some of the reasons for this are obvious enough. Its language is continuously

Alice Through the Looking-Glass by Lewis Carroll,
illustrated by John Tenniel

unexpected, impudent and daring—it is a great masterpiece of verbal absurdity: this is a quality which both adults and children appreciate from the moment they learn to regard language as an advanced game. The book goes on being entertaining because of its endless surprisingness. The situations Alice finds herself facing are also unexpected and ridiculous, but their delights would soon run out but for the ambiguous position of Alice herself. We never quite know who she is or how to take her. Is she a small and vulnerable girl, confronted with a sequence of disturbing crises—all the more disturbing because of their crackpot nature and rapid change? Or is she really an infant governess, the only adult in a childish world, dismayed by its eccentricities but always capable of applying her own good sense to sound, destructive effect? Should we be laughing at Alice's dream world or at Alice herself? What exactly *is* good sense, after all? Someone has obviously missed the point, but who? We can never be entirely sure of our ground. Nor can Alice, of course, but that is not to say that our problems are identical, or that we should see her as Heroine.

Perhaps no episode typifies the book's continuing fascination so clearly as the one in which Alice undergoes bewildering changes in her physical size and relation to her surroundings. The uncertainties we have about her nature are given physical expression by this incident, and it has parallels with both childhood and adult experience. For the child, the developing and changing sense of his own relationship with the external world, his fluctuating sense of subjection and control, helplessness and mastery, is given outward form in Alice's bewildering alternations. But fluctuations like this do not disappear entirely as one grows up—they merely take on different forms, perhaps more complex though less sharply felt. Most adults continue to oscillate between confidence and self-doubt, or feel at times that what is obviously rational is also ridiculous. Amongst other things, *Alice in Wonderland* gives perfect expression to the conflict between ourselves as self-contained, confident individuals, and the world around us which refuses to accept us as we are, or to confirm our own views of what is correct or important. In giving comic form to semi-permanent states of psychological disturbance, experienced by adults as well as children, the book repeatedly touches on zones of sensitivity that most of us, in some form, share. *Alice* does not cease to be a children's book because of this, but it is not *just* a children's book.

If we think particularly of the second part of the Alice story, *Through the Looking Glass*, we see in especially vivid form another of Carroll's preoccupations. This is, after all, a mathematician's work, and both books are repeatedly concerned with games of number, pattern, repetition, sequence, or codified word arrangements. Logic and the mockery of logic, rationalism and the absurdity of rationalism, the comic pleasures of the dance or the chessboard or other kinds of artificial order—these are intrinsic to the success of *Alice*. As we saw in talking of nursery rhymes, these are kinds of pleasure that begin in early childhood, but they continue into adult life. Similar preoccupations and pleasures are vital in the work of Samuel Beckett, notably *Waiting for Godot* and the novel *Murphy*: no one, however, suggests that we should see *him* as a writer for children!

If *Alice* has been purloined by adults, *Gulliver's Travels* has been partially lost to them. Interestingly, the two sections of the book which have always appealed most strongly to children—the voyages to Lilliput and Brobdingnag—depend like parts of *Alice* on powerful images of physical size. Lemuel Gulliver, the all-powerful giant in Lilliput, is the helpless midget of Brobdingnag. For Swift these physical changes are conscious attempts to find perspectives for humanity. Gulliver's physical diminution in Brobdingnag is an outward expression of his own moral inadequacy and that of his race: it leads to the King of Brobdingnag's famous denunciation of human kind: 'I cannot but conclude the bulk of your natives to be the most pernicious race of little odious vermin that nature ever suffered to crawl upon the surface of the earth.'

In the power of this statement we can see those dimensions of *Gulliver's Travels* which child readers are unlikely to appreciate or even notice: the intense revulsion against mankind, the over-

125

powering sense of physical and moral squalor. But this too is a book which exists at many levels, and its popularity is another indication of children's ability to ignore what does not concern them in an otherwise enticing book. The story is good. The situations are both exciting and funny; they include capture and escape and dangers. In all his fantastic predicaments Gulliver, like Alice, is convincingly ordinary. In his adventures there is the same alluring contrast of power and impotence. Here too we are never completely sure whose side we should be on. When qualities like these attract children to the story, they are obviously not reading it at the level of great satire, but they are not reading a mere adventure story either: as with *Alice*, there are points of connection between a child's reading and an adult's.

In modern writing these points of connection are most obvious in the work of J R R Tolkien—work which causes strong disagreements among both child and adult readers. *The Hobbit* is published as a children's book; the trilogy *The Lord of the Rings* as a work for adults. Although *The Hobbit* is certainly a much briefer and simpler story, the distinction is more of a publishing convenience than anything else—all the books draw their readers into the same strikingly imagined world.

In short, then, established classics form a special category mainly because they are books of confirmed distinction that we can offer to children with special pleasure and confidence. They do not comprise a worthy experience to which children should be forcibly introduced. Nothing is more likely to obstruct a child's pleasure in reading than a premature compulsory encounter with some classic work which his parents or teachers require him to approve. Until a very late stage in the development of mature understanding it is still true that when a great book is deliberately introduced by an adult, not accidentally discovered by the child, it is best to introduce it by reading aloud. This is the way most children come across Beatrix Potter or A A Milne, and it can just as easily be the way they come across Dickens. Dickens, of course, specialised in presenting his own work in this way, something which is worth remembering

by teachers or parents who feel with some sort of obscure guilti-
ness that by reading aloud they are being self-indulgent or
allowing children to be lazy. I can think of nothing which is
more calculated to awaken enjoyment of Dickens than listening
to a good, dramatic reading of the opening scene from *Great
Expectations*, preferably on a foul twilit afternoon near Christmas. Many other classics can be introduced or 'tasted' in this
way, and there is immediate audience reaction to tell us if the
time is ripe for them. Provided our own expectations are not
too great, and we are not deterred by failures, the practice of
reading excerpts in this way (and they can just as well be taken
from the middle of a book as from the beginning) can do
nothing but good.

Another way of avoiding deterrent veneration of the 'great
works' is to keep in mind how much they have in common with
other books which children enjoy. This is chiefly a question of
situations. Numerous popular modern stories depict children
coping with domestic crises, living through the temporary loss
or incapacity of parents, or finding that at times their parents
are themselves in need : living through such experiences, and in
the process coming to some kind of adult responsibility, is a
way of growing. *Little Women* or *The Railway Children* are
also about such times. Another standard situation—one which
we have noticed elsewhere—is that of being marooned, either
without conventional adult aid of any kind, or else with a family
group intact, but left to forage for itself in adverse circumstances. Although an island is the classic setting, it can just as
well be a forest or an area of wild country, or it can be a
country in the chaos of wartime, as in Ian Serraillier's *The
Silver Sword*, or even the heart of an industrial town, as in John
Rowe Townsend's *Gumble's Yard*. All such books can be
thought of as 'island situations', whether or not the waves are
breaking within earshot. The list of such books must also include
The Children of the New Forest, or *Treasure Island*, or *The
Swiss Family Robinson*; it must also include *Robinson Crusoe*.
In the classics as much as anywhere else, it is the situations
which must have power and meaning, and in books for children

it is quite possible to talk of a 'classic plot'. Anyone who doubts the importance of these stories might well remember that another island story, Ballantyne's *The Coral Island*, is a direct ancestor of the most famous and disturbing island story our own age has produced, William Golding's *Lord of the Flies*. Here is another book which can be read at many different levels, by both adults and younger readers. We do not yet know whether it will prove a 'classic novel'—but what matters most is that the book, despite its terrible implications, is widely enjoyed. The very notion of a 'classic novel' is a dangerous one if it deflects our attention from that.

BOOK-LIST OF THE CLASSICS

(See the note on pp. 37–39)

This list has three main sections. *Section One* covers one kind of 'classic' —the story derived from myth and legend, re-told or re-made. In this section I have included some books derived from the Bible, not because I see it as just another source of 'myth and legend', but because it contains so many great stories which have taken on the anonymity of multiple re-telling, and because in the present climate children who do not meet these stories in re-told versions may never meet them at all. *Section Two* lists some 'classic' stories which were always intended for children and are still widely enjoyed by them. *Section Three* lists some 'classic' novels which were initially written for adults, but which children have either appropriated over the years, or frequently enjoy in their original versions or in intelligent abridgements.

In *Section Two* are included the special case of Hans Andersen's and the Grimm Brothers' fairy stories.

First of all are listed some major series of children's classics.

Series

Oxford University Press: 'Oxford Illustrated Classics'.
This series includes a bit of everything: the fairy tales of Andersen and Grimm, some retold classics including Eleanor Farjeon's version of *Tales From Chaucer*, a 'children's classic' such as *The Swiss Family Robinson*, and an 'adult classic' in *Gulliver's Travels*. One or two individual volumes are also listed in the appropriate sections below.

Warne: 'Abridged classics for Upper Primary and Middle Schools'.
Includes *Great Expectations* and *Lorna Doone*. Opinions vary, but of their kind they are quite well done.

Blackie: 'Chosen Books'.
  This series is exceptionally good: selected, unadapted classics for children over ten, including *Little Women, King Solomon's Mines, Journey to the Centre of the Earth*.
Bodley Head: 'Nonesuch Cygnets'.
  Expensive and luxurious editions, beautifully produced—very much books for a special occasion. Includes *Alice* and *The Hunting of the Snark, Robinson Crusoe* (abridged, and illustrated by Edward Ardizzone), *Treasure Island, At The Back of the North Wind*, and E Nesbit's 'Bastables' stories.
Dent: 'Children's Illustrated Classics'.
  An extensive series, including *Tom Sawyer* and *Huckleberry Finn* (illustrated by C Walter Hodges), *Journey to the Centre of the Earth, Tom Brown's Schooldays, What Katy Did*.
Collins: 'Classics for Today'.
  All carefully abridged by skilled and reputable authors. Includes some interesting and unusual items, such as *White Fang*, George Macdonald's *The Princess and the Goblin* and *The Princess and Curdie*, and *The Moonstone*, as well as more obvious choices.

SECTION ONE

Two series of myth, legend and folk lore:

a) For older readers: 'Oxford myths and legends', Oxford.
b) For readers of 7–9: 'Folk Stories of the World', Oxford.

Jacynth Hope-Simpson	*The Hamish Hamilton Book of Myths and Legends*	Hamish Hamilton
Michael Brown	*The Hamish Hamilton Book of Sea Legends*	

Other, similar volumes are also available.

Michael Flanders	*Captain Noah and his Floating Zoo*	Collins
Reinhard Herrmann	*The Christmas Story Jonah and the Whale Noah's Ark*	Macmillan (Bible Picture Books)

See this series generally. The above are suitable for the youngest children, and for those only a little older:

George MacBeth	*Jonah and the Lord Noah's Journey*

For older readers:

James Reeves	*A First Bible* (linked passages from the Authorised Version)	Heinemann
	A Road to the Kingdom (stories from the Old and New Testaments)	
Ivan Southall	*The Sword of Esau* (Old Testament stories re-told)	Angus & Robertson
	The Curse of Cain (Old Testament stories re-told)	

Josephine Kamm	*A New Look at the Old Testament*	Gollancz
Rosemary Harris	*The Moon in the Cloud*	Faber
	The Shadow on the Sun	
	The Bright and Morning Star	

Rosemary Harris's trilogy, the first volume of which won the Carnegie Medal, is a brilliant example of how biblical story can be re-worked to fine effect. This section in general should provide a good introduction to the biblical inheritance. I have deliberately included several versions of the 'Noah' story, showing how it can be re-told for different age-groups. The boyhood of Jesus is beautifully reconstructed in

| Lavinia Derwent | *The Boy in the Bible* | Blackie |
| Mary Renault | *The Lion in the Gateway* | Kestrel |

a story of the Persian Wars

| Ian Serraillier | *The Way of Danger* | Oxford |

the life of Theseus re-told from Greek-myth

Amabel Williams-Ellis	*The Arabian Knights*	Blackie
Roger Lancelyn Green	*Tales of Ancient Egypt*	Bodley Head
James Reeves	*Heroes and Monsters: legends of Ancient Greece*	Blackie

Also issued in two volumes as *Gods and Voyagers* and *Islands and Palaces*.

Roger Lancelyn Green	*Heroes of Greece and Troy*	Bodley Head
Andrew Lang	*Tales of Greece and Troy*	Faber
Kathleen Lines (ed)	*The Faber Book of Greek Legends*	
Jacques le Marchand	*The Adventures of Ulysses*	
Edward Blishen and Leon Garfield	*The God Beneath the Sea*	Kestrel
	The Golden Shadow	

The Blishen and Garfield books are quite outstanding re-interpretations, with illustrations by Charles Keeping which are likely to acquire classic status on their own account.

Ian Serraillier	*Heracles the Strong*	Hamish Hamilton
Penelope Farmer and Graham McCallum	*The Story of Persephone*	Collins
Penelope Farmer and Chris Connor	*Daedalus and Icarus*	
Barbara Leonie Picard	*The Iliad of Homer*	Oxford

See also *The Heroes* below

James Reeves	*Fables from Aesop*	Blackie
Gaynor Chapman	*Aesop's Fables*	Hamish Hamilton
Barbara Leonie Picard	*Tales of the Norse Gods and Heroes*	Oxford
Henry Treece	*The Burning of Njal* adapted from the Icelandic sagas	Bodley Head
Roger Lancelyn Green	*Myths of the Norsemen*	
Alan Boucher	*The Sword of the Raven*	Kestrel
Ian Serraillier	*Havelok the Warrior*	Hamish Hamilton
Kevin Crossley-Holland	*Havelok the Dane*	Macmillan
Ian Serraillier	*Beowulf the Warrior*	Oxford
Rosemary Sutcliff	*Beowulf*	Bodley Head

The Puffin version of this book is entitled *Dragon Slayer*.

Robert Nye	*Bee Hunter: Adventures of Beowulf*	Faber
Pauline Clarke	*Torolv the Fatherless*	
Rosemary Sutcliff	*The High Deeds of Finn MacCool*	Bodley Head
	The Hound of Ulster	

Two re-tellings of Irish legend, the second dealing with the deeds of Cuchulain.

Barbara Leonie Picard	*Stories of King Arthur and his Knights*	Oxford
Roger Lancelyn Green	*King Arthur and his Knights of the Round Table*	Faber
Alice M Hadfield	*King Arthur and the Round Table*	Dent

and for older readers, the re-interpretations by T H White, the most famous of which is *The Sword in the Stone*, collected together in

T H White	*The Once and Future King*	Collins
Ian Serraillier	*The Challenge of the Green Knight*	Oxford
Rosemary Sutcliff	*The Chronicles of Robin Hood*	
Carola Oman	*Robin Hood*	Dent
Donald Suddaby	*Robin Hood Omnibus*	Blackie
Howard Pyle	*The Merry Adventures of Robin Hood*	Collins

See also Geoffrey Trease's *Bows Against the Barons*, Brockhampton.

Barbara Leonie Picard	*Hero Tales from the British Isles*	Kaye & Ward

SECTION TWO
Hans Andersen

	Hans Andersen's Fairy Tales, trans. L W Kingsland	Oxford
	Fairy Tales and Legends	Bodley Head

This edition is beautifully illustrated by Rex Whistler.

| Hans Andersen | *Forty-Two Stories,* trans. M R James | Faber |
| | *Stories from Hans Andersen,* abridged by Phillipa Pearce | Collins |

Some individual stories:

Hans Andersen	*The Tinderbox*	Methuen
	The Jumping Match	Hamish Hamilton
	The Steadfast Tin Soldier	

Brothers Grimm:

Brothers Grimm	*Complete Fairy Tales*	Longmans
	Fairy Tales	Cape
	Grimm's Fairy Tales	Blackie
	About Wise Men and Simpletons	Hamish Hamilton
Mervyn Peake illus.	*Household Tales*	Methuen
Amabel Williams-Ellis trans. Elizabeth Shub	*The Secret Shoemakers and other stories after Grimm*	Abelard-Schuman
James Reeves and Edward Ardizzone	*How the Moon Began*	

The remaining books in this list usually appear in a number of different editions, and particular publishers and series are noted only when they are specially recommended.

Lewis Carroll	*Alice's Adventures in Wonderland*	Macmillan (many other editions)
	Through the Looking Glass and What Alice Found There	Macmillan (many other editions)
Lewis Carroll, illus. Helen Oxenbury	*The Hunting of the Snark*	Heinemann
Lewis Carroll, illus. Mervyn Peake	*The Hunting of the Snark*	Chatto, Boyd & Oliver
Frances Hodgson Burnett	*The Secret Garden*	Heinemann
	Little Lord Fauntleroy	

The misleading reputation of this novel should not put one off: it is a very searching, well-written story.

E Nesbit	*The Lost Prince*	Hamish Hamilton
	The Railway Children	Benn
	The Story of the Treasure-Seekers	
	The House of Arden	
	Five Children and It	
J R Wyss	*The Swiss Family Robinson*	
George Macdonald, illus. E H Shepard	*At The Back of the North Wind*	Dent

George Macdonald, illus. D J Watkins-Pitchford	*The Lost Princess: a Double Story*	Dent
Captain Marryat	*The Children of the New Forest*	
Anna Sewell	*Black Beauty*	
F W Farrar	*Eric; or Little by Little*	Hamish Hamilton
R M Ballantyne	*The Coral Island*	
Susan Coolidge	*What Katy Did*	
Louisa M Alcott	*Little Women*	
	Good Wives	
	Jo's Boys	
	Little Men	
Charles Kingsley	*The Water Babies*	
	The Heroes	

This book is one of the early major re-tellings of ancient myth.

R L Stevenson	*Treasure Island*	
Mark Twain	*Tom Sawyer*	
Thomas Hughes	*Tom Brown's Schooldays*	Hamish Hamilton
Richard Jefferies, illus. E H Shepard	*Bevis*	Cape
Kenneth Grahame	*The Wind in the Willows*	Methuen

Various editions are available, differing in format and illustrations. The line drawings by E H Shepard are not, in my view, excelled by the colour illustrations of either Arthur Rackham or Shepard himself.

L M Montgomery	*Anne of Green Gables*	Harrap
Rudyard Kipling	*The Jungle Book*	Macmillan
	Just So Stories	
	Puck of Pook's Hill	
	Rewards and Fairies	
Walter de la Mare	*Collected Stories for Children*	Faber

SECTION THREE

James Reeves (adapted); Edward Ardizzone (illus.) from Cervantes:

	Exploits of Don Quixote	
Daniel Defoe	*Robinson Crusoe*	
Swift	*Gulliver's Travels*	
Sir Walter Scott	*Ivanhoe*	
Charlotte Bronte	*Jane Eyre*	
Dickens	*Great Expectations*	
Mark Twain	*Huckleberry Finn*	
Stephen Crane	*The Red Badge of Courage*	
Jules Verne	*20,000 Leagues Under the Sea*	
	Round the World in Eighty Days	
	Journey to the Centre of the Earth	

R D Blackmore	*Lorna Doone*	
Rider Haggard	*King Solomon's Mines*	
Rudyard Kipling	*Kim*	Macmillan
J Meade Falkner	*Moonfleet*	Arnold

And two 'classic' school stories for readers with such tastes:

| Talbot Baines Reed | *The Fifth Form at St Dominic's* | Hamish Hamilton |
| Rudyard Kipling | *Stalky and Co* | Macmillan |

8 Adolescent Reading

From the age of thirteen onwards young readers will turn increasingly to books published for adults, especially to popular fiction by such writers as Mary Stewart, Alistair Maclean, Margery Allingham or Nevil Shute. Between thirteen and sixteen there are important formative years in which the need for a special literature has largely faded, and the interests and problems of adult life can best be met from the adult library. In any case, this is a notoriously difficult age-group to write for, and there are not very many outstanding books which were written with adolescents specially in mind. Of the ones there are, we can say with even more confidence than we did at earlier stages that adults are likely to enjoy them just as much.

This gradual movement towards adult fiction does not mean that there is no need at all for a more specific adolescent literature, only that good books for this level are scarcer and should be valued highly. In particular there are perhaps three major adolescent concerns where good novels can help : the beginning of important sexual relations, of work, and of sensitive (though often hidden) class consciousness. Of course sex and social class are common preoccupations well before thirteen, but at this stage they take on a more active presence and capacity to hurt.

The perils of sexuality were dealt with frequently in Victorian children's fiction, often with such dark allusions to perversion, and such harping on obscure causes for guilt and shame that they must have caused more alarm and mystification than reassurance or enlightenment. The alternative stratagem, more widespread and long-lasting in fiction for children, was a coy assumption that the human body remains boisterously neuter until the age of twenty-five or thereabouts.

In recent years a saner practice has gradually established itself, and responsible acceptance of sexuality is no longer a taboo subject in adolescent fiction. For this we owe a particular debt to Geoffrey Trease, who by precept and example has done much to open a new dimension in modern writing. Trease made some pioneering efforts to engage with the realities of adolescence, and the fact that some of his work now seems dated and mildly embarrassing is largely attributable to his own achievements. The most important set of books that Trease produced in modern settings was the 'Black Banner' series, which records the adventures of a group of boys and girls attending grammar schools in a small lakeland town. His characters do not have the fictitious child's remarkable gift for remaining permanently fixed at the same age; they grow older, and from book to book the relationships between them deepen and change.

The 'Black Banner' series is perhaps the most authentic portrait in fiction of the post-war grammar school ethos, and the life-style of its approved pupils. The boys and girls of these books are decent, humorous and self-reliant, respectfully tolerant of their teachers but hardly over-awed, accepting cheerfully the conventions of both school and home, responsible and sensibly ambitious. Their growing sexual awareness and its problems is placed in an everyday context of amateur dramatics, sports days, school trips, and hiking. As a project the whole series is admirable and has enjoyed deserved popularity.

But although the books are still a readable yarn, time has really passed them by. Towards the end of the series, in *Black Banner Abroad*, the main characters—now in advanced adolescence—accompany a school party taking a play production to France, and the narrator, Bill, falls heavily for a French girl staying with relatives in the house where he is boarded. Alas, the end of the holiday brings separation, but on the train home Bill overhears a conversation in which the true nature of his French beloved is revealed: if she isn't jolly careful, one day she will be a loose woman. This shocking revelation is enough to deflect Bill back on to the path of true love—a growing affection for his school-friend Penny, with whom it has long been clear that he will enjoy ultimate bliss.

The trouble is, of course, that life is not like that, or not often, and there is about these well-intentioned books a faintly embarrassing tone which now seems just as obsolete as the prim evasions they set out to displace. Adolescent sexuality is not so readily accommodated within a general decency, or so easily controlled by a clockwork moral system. And largely because of Trease's own efforts, there are writers who have been able to develop this theme much further.

Here, for example, is Christina, the heroine of K M Peyton's *Flambards*, watching the servant Violet helping her handsome cousin Mark, who has bloodied his nose out hunting :

'Christina, drying herself by the fire, looked up through the tangled curtain of her hair and saw Violet take the things to Mark, and stand by him with a towel. Her face . . . seemed to shine with sympathy; her big green eyes were filled with a tenderness that shocked Christina. "Why, she—she—" Christina's mind struggled with a conception completely new to her. She remembered Violet saying that Mark was handsome, but it had never occurred to her that Violet could—could— Christina could not even acknowledge that there was a name for Violet's feelings, so transparently evident as she stood over Mark. She was suddenly quite furious, crouched there beside the fire. She threw her hair back and stood up quickly. "Violet, take some hot water up to my room." She spoke with a sharpness that made Violet jump.
"Yes, miss."
Christina went upstairs feeling utterly confused. "Why did I speak like that?" she wondered, for how could anyone be jealous of Violet? Christina did not know. She felt angry and upset, and all for no reason that she understood.'

Flambards, the first novel in a distinguished trilogy, is set in the period 1908–1912. It is a period when servants like Violet were servants, and Christina is an heiress, farmed out with ulterior motives to impoverished relations who are mostly obsessed by hunting. Later in the novel Violet becomes pregnant by Mark and is dismissed. As a direct result her invalid mother dies in the workhouse. Mark is severely beaten up by Violet's brother, a beating with which no one interferes.

Flambards by K M Peyton, illustrated by Victor Ambrus

It is all very different from the tone which Trease judged appropriate in his books of a few years earlier: more violent, more ruthless, more passionate, more complicated. Christina's confusion is the acutely recorded symptom of painful and bewildering extensions of feeling, and it is handled with delicacy but without evasion. The whole novel displays equivalent candour and insight. Nothing is wilfully sensational, but nothing is watered down.

Flambards is one book which accepts, so to speak, Trease's contention that sex is a vital part of adolescence and should not be avoided, but does not accept that it can be quietly slotted into the spectrum of teenage experience on the same level as sport, or as just a significant deepening of friendship. Instead, in K M Peyton's work the tension, upheaval and uncertainties are given their full weight and pressure. One distinguished feature of *Flambards* (and there are others) is its power to go right to the centre of adolescent sexual doubt and communicate its exhilaration as sharply as its pain.

This deservedly popular novel illustrates a visible trend in some recent books for teenage readers. Not only does it successfully incorporate within the story a vivid account of sexual awakening and early experience, but the story itself has a larger imaginative coherence. That is to say, the novel is in no sense a pretext for exploring adolescent trials; instead, the trials are necessary and even inevitable in terms of the plot. The book is other things besides a history of adolescent growth : it is also social history, and shows how unobtrusive and yet absorbing the 'history' in a good historical novel can be. The period is one which has particular attractions for modern readers—it is very remote from contemporary experience, yet it falls within the lifetime and the memories of many living grandparents of today's adolescents; it describes a vanished world, dominated by the horse, in the act of vanishing, and being overtaken by the mechanical revolution of cars and aeroplanes. In short, it is placed at a vital junction of time, the point at which our own material world came fully into existence. The tensions generated between the characters—not only the adolescent ones—emerge directly from the historical tensions of their period, and in their turmoil of private feelings they are not merely having to choose between bewildering emotional drives, but also to choose half-consciously between one world, one way of life, and another.

Conflicting ways of life involve not only the rights and wrongs of animals as against sundry mechanical contraptions, but the rights and wrongs of the way society is organised. The most striking social observation in the novel is the plain fact that at

Flambards horses are treated better than people. Admittedly when a horse has served its turn it becomes a few pounds-worth of dog-meat, but human beings who have served their turn fare little better. Horses are kept in clean warm stables and dosed with brandy, while a bedridden widow-woman decays in a hovel. Dismissal without references means hopeless unemployment, and leads in turn to crime. The beginning of a natural warm relationship between Christina and the stable-boy Dick, who teaches her to ride, is blocked by the social barrier between them. Later in the series it is a sign of the crumbling social walls that the obstacles between these two are no longer insurmountable. *Flambards* is—in part—a highly intelligent and revealing analysis of class-consciousness and the motives that make or break it.

Divisions in society are bound up with a clear sense of work —of the problems of getting it and keeping it, the weariness and difficulty of doing it without the heart's consent, the thrill of doing it because the will and the interest match the need, and the dangers and consequences of losing it. Here too the book has much to say—entirely within the terms of the story and without exterior preaching—about the nature of work, effort and reward.

It is ironical perhaps that on top of all this *Flambards* manages to be the pony story to end all pony stories. The horses in this novel are not the stuff of daydreams but real beasts, commanding strong feelings in their owners and riders which are governed by the varied nature and temperament of the horses themselves, who in their way are individualised quite as sharply as the human characters—yet their power to excite strong feelings does not lead to sentimentality, because it is always accompanied by a realistic evaluation of both the horse and the way it is treated.

Flambards, then, has just about everything. Like the other books which I include in this section, it could perfectly well be read by younger people, and often is. But it belongs here as a first-rate story which repeatedly touches on the deepest concerns of adolescent readers, and does so with the power to evoke that stir of familiarity and self-recognition which is so valuable a part of childhood and adolescent reading.

Throughout this book I have emphasised the importance of fantasy, not as an escape into the delusive comforts of a never-never-land, but as a format for important kinds of realism. It is a great mistake to think of realism and fantasy as opposites. The kind of fantasy which provides a vehicle for realistic treatment of emotional growth is another valuable experience for readers in their teens, and the appearance of successful books in this genre is another encouraging sign that writers are finding it possible to explore emergent sexuality without embarrassment or didacticism. The most celebrated book of this kind is probably Alan Garner's *The Owl Service*.

The plot of *The Owl Service* concerns the re-enactment of a Welsh legend in the lives of three modern adolescents—Roger, Alison and Gwyn. Roger and Alison, step-brother and step-sister in the aftermath of earlier marital wreck, are middle-class English adolescents on holiday in Wales; Gwyn is the clever, grammar-school offspring of the local housekeeper, Nancy. Each of the three has a part to play in the tragic repetition of the old legend of love and betrayal, which works itself out anew in succeeding generations.

Garner, whose three earlier novels were written for younger readers, is best-known as a writer of fantasy, particularly interested in the sudden incursion of disturbing extra-natural events into the placid everyday lives of present-day children, and *The Owl Service* has been much admired for its compulsive underswell of supernatural forces. Certainly the book is an intriguing and impressive achievement, a unique book which defies classification, except that it obviously has a great deal to offer to readers in this age-group. Yet oddly enough the fantasy which underpins the plot is probably the least satisfactory aspect of the book. Technically, it is handled in a way which, by Garner's own standards, is crude and maladroit, the legend itself being inserted in 'gobbet' form rather than woven into the flow of the story. Furthermore, the parallelism between the legendary figures and the modern children is far from clear. It could be

141

argued that this is justifiably intentioned, since it certainly contributes to an exciting and astonishing conclusion, and the many readers who enjoy this book seem fairly unworried by it. But the novel does seem to demand a rather less misty design than it actually has: I have discussed it with a number of student-teachers who were almost all agreed in admiring the book, but in a state of dispute and uncertainty about its meaning and its underlying coherence.

What *does* undoubtedly succeed is the impressive atmospheric creation which is built up through the book, not so much from its legendary origin but from the images and presences deriving from it—the pervasive shadowy influence of owls and meadow-sweet, and of extensions of the legend through modernistic symbols, especially the motor-bike. Against this heavy, intense and obscure background is played out the triangle of modern adolescent conflict, and it is here that *The Owl Service* works most triumphantly. Alison is the focus of a strong, harsh, emotionally cruel conflict between Roger and Gwyn, a conflict of profound subterranean bitterness beneath a surface of cutting, satiric raillery or patches of uneasy truce. The conflict is marked by the same kind of insight on the author's part that we found in *Flambards*: a recognition that sexual tensions and rivalries cannot be extricated from the tangle of other sensitivities which characterise adolescent growth. Roger and Gwyn are each the children of unhappy unions and parental inadequacy, and each is burdened with a parent he despises—each, therefore, has a problem of emergent identity which is explosive material when they meet and confront each other. Its dangers are increased by other accidents: each boy is clever, but clever in a vacuum, too clever for the task of unaided survival. And the similarities of their situations are set against dangerous opposites: English and Welsh, native and alien, privileged middle-class and deprived proletarian, cosmopolitan and parochial. The conflict takes its special quality from the fact that Gwyn and Roger are old and intelligent enough to have some sharp intermittent understanding of these things, but not enough to give them control over their lives. Sexual jealousy is entwined with all this. Garner's

142

treatment of these relationships is harsh and powerful, and his handling of dialogue, especially of highly-motivated adolescent wit, is masterly. *The Owl Service* is not a complete artistic success, but it is a remarkable and important book.

Another recent novel, John Gordon's *The House on the Brink*, is also a strange and intriguing achievement in which the background fantasy is somewhat blurred in comparison with its sharp foreground treatment of emotional relationships. Apparently less well-known than either of these, and certainly less well-known than it deserves to be, is Rosemary Harris's *The Seal-Singing*, which deals—like *The Owl Service*—with the working-out through a trio of modern adolescents of a bygone tragedy, this time one which has assumed the quality of legend from roots of fact. *The Seal-Singing*, the story of a Scottish island and its seal-colony, is in my view a much more consistent and assured artistic success than *The Owl Service*. The 'legend' in this case is immaculately rendered into the modern story, and matched with great precision and subtlety against the emotional realities of the modern characters. The characterisation, though less heavily underscored and dramatic than Garner's, is more completely convincing. Comparisons are apt because there are some remarkable similarities between the two novels. In *The Seal-Singing* the Scottish cousins Toby and Catriona, who spend their holidays in Carrigona, are joined in mutually unwilling holiday companionship by their sophisticated and supposedly hardened cousin Miranda. Miranda's affinity of nature with the long-dead Lucy re-activates the sleeping tragedy of a time when Carrigona's seals were betrayed in their sanctuary, and the sad, treacherous Lucy died in the betraying. How Miranda awoke the ghost, and came ultimately to be the means of giving her a final rest, is a story which runs parallel with a harsh adolescent crisis. Here too there are differences of background and habit, social tensions, problems arising from the need to cope with things unaided, which give a precise sociological framework to the sexual needs and desires and hopes, the varied consciousness of emerging love, which are associated with them. And as in *The Owl Service*, the poetry of legend and of emotional awakening is offset by tough and steady humour. Neither book is by any means faultless, but their appearance is a valuable contribution to the literature of adolescent experience.

Lastly, at least a brief mention must be made of another 'unclassifiable' book—a remarkable fantasy which might be enjoyed by quite young children, and which certainly has much to offer to adult readers, but seems specially appropriate in the period of adolescent emergence. This is Ursula Le Guin's *A Wizard of Earthsea*, a beautifully written story which is perhaps a new classic. It is the story of an imaginary world of scattered islands in which great power for good is entrusted to magicians, trained by a magician-priesthood on their island-fastness of Roke. A young magician, Ged, a boy gifted with extraordinary powers, comes to Roke for his training, but by irresponsible use of his gifts he releases into the world a destructive force of nameless evil. How Ged was first pursued by the evil he unleashed, how he became the hunter instead of the hunted, and how at last he faced the evil and gave it its name, so winning his freedom and his mastery—this is the theme of the novel. It descends from all legends of exile and heroic quest, and mingles with this classic theme a tense and moving history of guilt and expiation, of youthful pride and recklessness redeemed by courage and suffering, of fundamental experiences in the quest which everyone must undertake, in search of self-knowledge and stable identity. In the magic and the realism and the profound psychological truth of this magnificent book, many of the themes we have touched on in these chapters are brought together and given a most profound expression. The two later novels which recount the further adventures of Ged, *The Tombs of Atuan* and *The Farthest Shore*, are in no way inferior, and the series forms one of the outstanding achievements in contemporary fiction for young people.

The Spirit of Jem by P H Newby,
illustrated by Keith Vaughan

BOOK-LIST FOR ADOLESCENT READING

(See the note on pp. 37–39)

This is a difficult though important area of fiction for young readers. In compiling the list below I have assumed that many readers will still be enjoying books aimed partly at younger age-groups, and many (including the same ones, since interests fluctuate so greatly) will also be choosing adult fiction. The books listed here do not form an autonomous category between these two extremes—many of them could well be enjoyed by adult readers, and could indeed have been published for an adult readership in the first place. They do, however, touch repeatedly on topics of special interest to adolescents—love, sexual attraction and its possible consequences, family relationships, tensions and conflicts, social problems which are likely to arise at first-hand or become important even when they are not experienced directly, questions of illness and disablement, and fundamental issues of moral or political choice. The historical novels listed here often deal with such problems, and hence are fully 'modern' in their interests. I hope, however, that the list is not too solemn as a result: its over-riding concern is to offer a choice of novels which are absorbing and exciting in their own right, and by no means all of them are 'serious' in the way this note might suggest.

Zvi Libne (Lieberman)	*In The Beginning* *The Children of the Cave*	Oxford

Two novels of early Jewish history.

Stephanie Plowman	*The Road to Sardis*	Bodley Head
Hans Baumann	*Sons of the Steppe*	Oxford
Rosemary Sutcliff	*The Lantern Bearers*	

Of all Rosemary Sutcliff's novels dealing with the aftermath of the Roman Empire, this is the one which is particularly appropriate for older readers.

Rosemary Sutcliff	*The Mark of the Horse Lord*	Oxford
	The Rider of the White Horse	Hodder
Winifred Cawley	*Feast of the Serpent*	Oxford

A novel touching on trial for witchcraft at the time of the Civil War.

Geoffrey Trease	*Horsemen on the Hills*	Macmillan

A novel dealing with some of the harsher realities of Renaissance Italy.

E M Almedingen	*Anna*	Oxford
Hester **Burton**	*Time of Trial*	
	Thomas	

A novel of the Great Plague.

	The Rebel
	Riders of the Storm

A novel following up the consequences of the French Revolution.

Leon Garfield and   *Child o' War*   Collins
  David Proctor

> Not (sad to say) completely fictitious. A part-fictitious, part-documentary account of a young boy's involvement in sea-warfare during the Napoleonic Wars. Sometimes very funny, sometimes bitterly realistic, always morally intelligent—a short, powerful and important book.

Fay Goldie   *River of Gold*   Oxford
Harold Keith   *Komantcia*

> A novel of enslavement by the Comanches.

Stephanie   *Three Lives for the Czar*   Bodley Head
  Plowman   *My Kingdom for a Grave*

> Two novels set in the pre-revolutionary Russia of Czar Nicholas II.

Mary Graveston   *A Stone For My Keepsake*

> The first twenty are in some sense 'historical novels', provided the term is not used in a limiting way. They all have plenty to say which is relevant to modern readers. So do the books in the following groups of *fantasies* and *science fiction*:

Ursula le Guin   *A Wizard of Earthsea*   Gollancz
                 The Tombs of Atuan
                 The Farthest Shore
Joan Lingard   *The Clearance*   Hamish Hamilton
Leon Garfield   *The Strange Affair of*   Kestrel
                   Adelaide Harris

Historical farce; quite unlike Garfield's earlier books.

Richard Adams   *Watership Down*   Rex Collings
Alan Garner   *The Owl Service*   Collins
                 Red Shift
John Gordon   *The House on the Brink*   Hutchinson
Robert A Heinlein *Red Planet*   Gollancz
Lester del Rey   *Outpost of Jupiter*
Robert Gilman   *The Rebel of Rhada*
                 The Navigator of Rhada

> Gilman's two books may be particularly interesting for readers who like the work of Peter Dickinson and John Christopher (see pp. 100–101).

Andre Norton   *The X Factor*   Gollancz
                 Dread Companion

Some novels of special interest to readers concerned with the ideology and moral dimensions of politics:

J M Marks   *Ayo Gurkha*   Oxford
                 The Snow-Lion
                 Jason

147

P H Newby   *The Spirit of Jem*   Kestrel

A brilliant novel about the mechanics of totalitarianism, beautifully illustrated by Keith Vaughan.

John Branfield   *Nancekuke*   Gollancz

(Nancekuke is the Cornish centre for research into methods of chemical warfare.)

Hans Peter
  Richter, trans.
  Edite Kroll   *Friedrich*   Kestrel

Germany in the early 1930s. The growth of Nazism affects the friendship of two boys, one of whom is Jewish.

I Was There

Membership of Hitler Youth, followed by active service.

Alexander Cordell   *The Traitor Within*   Brockhampton
  Red China today.

Elliott Arnold   *A Kind of Secret Weapon*   Kestrel

The weapon in question is an underground newspaper.

J M Couper   *The Thundering Good Today*   Bodley Head

The 'Flambards' trilogy:

K M Peyton   *Flambards*   Oxford
                  The Edge of the Cloud
                  Flambards in Summer

Set a few years earlier, at the turn of the century is:

K M Peyton   *The Maplin Bird*   Oxford

A pair of novels dealing humorously and imaginatively with modern adolescent problems:

            Pennington's Seventeenth
            Summer
            The Beethoven Medal

and a parent-child clash over the choice of a career, in the context of illness:

            A Pattern of Roses

In all, these novels represent the most distinguished single contribution to adolescent literature by any author in recent years.

A collection of problems:

These novels cover a variety of adolescent difficulties, and I have not attempted to categorise them—partly because they are all important, partly because most of the books deal (inevitably) with more than one at once:

Josephine Kamm   *Young Mother*   Brockhampton

Historically this is an important novel, the first to deal outspokenly with sensitive issues which had long been suppressed in fiction for young readers. The same author has taken the theme of work in

First Job

148

and of race in

Out of Step

Amongst books which deal sensitively and well with emotional involvement are:

John Rowe Townsend	*The Summer People*	Oxford
Rosemary Harris	*The Seal-Singing*	Faber
Peggy Woodford	*Please Don't Go*	Bodley Head
Ruth Tomalin	*Away to the West*	Faber
Jill Chaney	*Return to Mottram Park*	Dobson
Julius Lester	*Two Love Stories*	Kestrel
Vera and Bill Cleaver	*Ellen Grae and Lady Ellen Grae Grover*	Hamish Hamilton

and, although I have reservations about them which are expressed on pp. 136–137, I respect the clarity and directness of

Geoffrey Trease	*Black Banner Abroad* *The Gates of Bannerdale*	Heinemann

A host of problems are covered by Paul Zindel, in books which clearly owe much to the influence of J D Salinger's *The Catcher in the Rye*. Opinions differ about them. My own is not enthusiastic, but the books are sufficiently respected, and so obviously relevant to teenage concerns, that they deserve some mention:

Paul Zindel	*The Pigman*	Bodley Head and others
	My Darling, My Hamburger *I Never Loved Your Mind*	Bodley Head

Other books of considerable interest include:

John Rowe Townsend	*Goodnight, Prof. Love*	Oxford
	The Intruder	
Joyce Cary	*Charley is my Darling*	Michael Joseph
Jill Paton Walsh	*Fireweed*	Macmillan

A novel which deals well with questions of social class.

Bo Carpelan	*The Wide Wings of Summer*	Heinemann
Joan G Robinson	*Charley*	Collins
Stanley Watts	*The Breaking of Arnold*	Kestrel
Margaret Storey	*Wrong Gear*	Faber
Malcolm Saville	*The Purple Valley*	Heinemann
Honor Arundel	*The Longest Weekend*	Hamish Hamilton

Saville's book explores the problem of drugs, Honor Arundel's that of pre-marital pregnancy. See also

Honor Arundel	*The Blanket Word*	Hamish Hamilton

Ray Pope   *Is It Always Like This?*   Macdonald

Ray Pope's book deals with problems of race. See also *Out of Step*. It is worth remembering that the greatest treatment of racial questions in all literature is

Mark Twain	*Huckleberry Finn*	
H F Brinsmead	*Beat of the City*	Oxford
	Listen to the Wind	
J M Couper	*Looking for a Wave*	Bodley Head
Mollie Hunter	*A Sound of Chariots*	Hamish Hamilton
Margaret J. Baker	*Prickets Way*	Methuen
Michael Hardcastle	*Don't Tell Me What To Do*	Heinemann
Ivan Southall	*To The Wild Sky*	Angus & Robertson
Brian Fairfax-Lucy and Philippa Pearce	*The Children of the House*	Kestrel

And several more recommended books and authors:

Scott O'Dell	*Island of the Blue Dolphins*	Kestrel
	The Black Pearl	
	The Dark Canoe	
Vian Smith	*Come Down the Mountain*	
	The Horses of Petrock	
Mabel Esther Allan	*Climbing to Danger*	Heinemann
	It Happened in Arles	
Stephen Chance	*Septimus and the Danedyke Mystery*	Bodley Head
	Septimus and the Minster Ghost	
Martin Ballard	*Dockie*	Kestrel
Vivian Breck	*Maggie*	
Geraldine Symons	*Mademoiselle*	Macmillan
Sally Bicknell	*The Midwinter Violins*	Chatto and Windus

A note on series

There is still a shortage of carefully selected series-lists for adolescent readers. Four deserve special mention. The Bodley Head's 'Books for New Adults' and Heinemann's 'Pyramid' books, the second of which are specially aimed at attracting non-habitual readers, are both excellent series from which a number of titles have been chosen for the above list. Macmillan's 'Topliner' books are paperbacks, and so fall outside the immediate scope of this list, but they include a number of excellent books specially written for the series. 'Topliners' are generally well-chosen, attractively produced and cheap; it is well worth keeping up to date with them. Penguin's 'Peacock' books, designed specifically for this age-group, have never quite flourished as might have been expected, but remain a useful venture in an area where there is little competition. 'Peacock' books do not approach the variety and excellence of 'Puffins', but the series should nevertheless be regularly checked for interesting additions.

Part Three

9 A Contrast of Problems: Enid Blyton and William Mayne

There are two areas of children's reading which tend to arouse particularly strong feelings. One is the comic, and the other is the work of Enid Blyton, a phenomenon of such proportions that it deserves some attention here and now.

For those who disapprove of Enid Blyton's work the facts are comfortless. Her books enjoy huge popularity with children over a wide age-range. It is not uncommon for public libraries to exclude Blytons from the list of books that children can reserve, because the creation of a waiting-list would cause bureaucratic problems of awesome dimensions. Moreover, once the taste has been established it has an almost inexhaustible supply of food— the only problem is the number of spoons to be plunged into the same dish. The indefatigable Miss Blyton widened the meaning of 'productivity' to a degree which the most hectoring politicians have not yet noticed. Alas for all these words and all these people who want to read them, there is a widespread view that they are undesirable words, and should be left unread. Now here is a problem indeed : who is wrong, the disapproving adult or the enthusiastic child? Surely, when the cleavage of opinion is as wide as this, *somebody* must be wrong. Why should we disapprove of something which children find so enticing?

Many accusations have been made, but these are prominent ones : Blyton's language is over-simplified, narcotically rhythmic, repetitive and lifeless—'readable' to a point where readability becomes a sin; her characters are pasteboard, and her child-protagonists often extremely nasty; her stories, such as those in the 'Famous Five' and 'Secret Seven' series, are based on stereotyped plots with a rusty apparatus of old houses, secret passages, stolen documents and faithful pets; her books frequently appeal to snobbishness and truculent aggressiveness; she propagates the unseemly notion that most adults are stupid; and there is *always* a happy ending.

Some of these criticisms can be easily dismissed. The stupidity of adults, for example, is a conventional device for releasing children into unsupervised activity where things can happen, and is used by the most respected writers; in general, children do not really believe it but find it a useful temporary supposition, both in their reading and their daily lives. Others have much greater force: for example, while it is undeniable that most children are frequently quarrelsome and spiteful, they tend to outgrow the worst of these faults long before the age when they are still routine behaviour for Blyton children, and it scarcely helps to depict them as virtues. Likewise, children can of course be intensely snobbish, but the usual form of this is a fairly harmless group-clannishness unless it is reinforced by adult support: Blyton books often provide such support. In short, the Blyton stories do tend to condone the least attractive ethical practices of schoolchildren, and their implied support for sundry kinds of anti-social behaviour is, in my view, their worst feature.

The criticism of Blyton's style, however, is the most important of all. Certainly the language is undemanding, being pitched at a reading-age several years below the age-group for which the book is ostensibly written. The books can be read at a quite amazing speed. But it would be hard to say that they are *badly* written, as compared with the bulk of children's fiction: the Blyton style is crisp and economical, and not over-packed with clichés—it is just very simple. Now at a certain stage in a child's reading development this can be a major virtue. A child who discovers that he can romp through these yarns at such a spanking pace may gain a great deal of confidence from doing so, and a wholly beneficial tendency to regard the pleasure of books as something which outweighs the bother.

If we want children to go on to find deeper and more complex pleasures in fiction, the real problem is not to steer them clear of Blyton, which is not only a hopeless task but one which may set up destructive resistances. For parent or teacher to express open disapproval of Blyton's work is tactless and mis-guided. The problem is to open the way to richer experiences without pouring scorn on the current idol. Various ways of doing this were described by a number of teachers in *The Use of English*, Vol. 18 Number 1 (Autumn 1966), responding to a request for ways of 'weaning' children off Blyton. Despite the fact that some of the 'children' are well into adolescence, the most useful contributions display a tolerance and lack of worry which I share and recommend. Mr D W Crompton suggests that if the most drastic of 'weaning' processes should fail, 'the alternative of letting well alone and praising be that they are reading anything at all might yet, in the long run, prove an equally satisfactory solution', and he is echoed by Mrs E Hesk, who says, 'To find that fifteen-year-old girls are still reading Enid Blyton is perhaps not so alarming as to find that they do not read at all, or that they favour the lurid type of teen-age magazine prevalent today.'

For parents and teachers alike, then, the Blyton phenomenon does not call for strong reactions—only a quiet strategy of presentation which should gradually produce results.

In thinking about the Blyton phenomenon it is salutary to remember that it has its opposite : the book which is admired and highly-praised by adults but does not arouse in most children the kind of enthusiasm it is held to deserve. Omission from the book-lists which follow certain chapters in this book does not necessarily mean that I believe the writer concerned to produce such books : the lists are designed to be highly selective, and exclude much that I value. But there is one writer whose exclusion is based on this reason, and whose case is so interesting that it needs some comment. This is William Mayne.

Mayne is a prolific and highly-esteemed writer for children, whose work is published in very attractive editions. It contains, in terms of plot and incident, a most exciting blend of traditional ingredients and contemporary settings. There are supernatural events, mysterious strangers, feuds, tunnels, caves and passages;

there is buried treasure. There are haunting and disturbing problems, solved with much ingenuity of plotting and in ways which are meaningful in terms of character as well as story. There are recognisable and realistic settings, extremely varied in nature and based on first-hand observation vividly recalled. There is, in many of the stories, a balance between home and school which does, I think, accurately reflect the daily experience of many children. There is also a more exotic and unusual scholastic setting, namely the Cathedral choir school which provides the background for some of Mayne's best-known books, *A Swarm in May*, *Cathedral Wednesday* and *Choristers' Cake*, and which has an offering of eccentric schoolmasters to set alongside the refreshingly normal and human versions who appear in other books—in fact Mayne has probably made a more imaginative and vigorous assault on the cliché-ridden school story than any other modern novelist. Any writer whose armoury includes both the comic-serious, candle-lit ritual world of *A Swarm in May*, and the bleak, bony landscape of *Ravensgill*, with its obscure violence and death, is endowed with remarkable versatility and richness of material. Mayne has a sharp sense of place and of character, a feeling for both comedy and high drama, a tonal scale which includes both supernatural enchantment and uncompromising realism.

In the last year or two particularly, the element of realism in Mayne's writing would justify, I think, some equivalent criticism to that which I have elsewhere directed at the work of Ivan Southall. But somehow, in my own experience—which may well be accidentally unrepresentative—the problem does not really arise, for the embarrassing reason that these formidable talents leave many children cold, although undoubtedly there are plenty of others who appreciate them.

The reasons why Mayne's books fail with children more often than they should are not easy to determine, but their lack of compromise must surely have much to do with it. In Enid Blyton the compromise is unceasing: there was never a writer more obedient to her market. Mayne's books, on the other hand, repeatedly show a strong inner withdrawal from their apparent surface compromise. When summarised, they contain the staple contents of children's stories, but they go on to interpose obstacles between the promise and the achievement. Mayne's style is admittedly difficult: his admirers concede that it is frequently elusive, elliptical, subtle. So indeed it is, and these are (or can be) virtues, if they impart an originality of tone and approach which reinvigorates hackneyed situations. But the real effect is different from this. The style of a Mayne novel operates as a form of continuous subdued recoil against the narrative shape and impetus which his plots demand, and the effect is a kind of obstructive fastidiousness in the writing which repeatedly devalues the dramatic and psychological crises of his stories.

For children who can respond to such complex and multiple demands, Mayne has much to offer. In my experience, and not to my surprise, such children are not a majority of habitual readers. It is common to hear good writers for children declare that they write as they must, to please themselves, and happen to publish in the child-market. More often than not this is all to the good, producing intelligent, uncondescending books which children enjoy, which adults could enjoy equally, and which make nonsense of 'children's book' as a classifying term. William Mayne is a writer of whom, I think, the broad description is true but the results are not beneficial; he is rightly admired by adults for qualities of imagination which are intensely interesting to the adult mind, and it is perhaps a very great pity that a highly individual concern for 'juvenile themes' should have been identified with a juvenile readership. Mayne's work poses in a most absorbing way, the question 'What are the qualities of a good novel for children?'

It is clear that we face an awkward dilemma. There is almost no limit to the reasons we could give for describing William Mayne's work as more distinguished than Enid Blyton's, but they are mostly reasons which we give as adult readers and critics, and arise partly from interests which Mayne has generated in ourselves. The awkward fact remains that far more children derive pleasure from Enid Blyton, and whatever reservations we may have about the kind of pleasure she gives, we cannot afford to deride it. If we do, we have stopped considering how to widen children's tastes, and instead begun to disregard them.

10 The World of the Comic: Aaargh!'

'Examination of a large number of these papers shows that, putting aside school stories, the favourite subjects are Wild West, Frozen North, Foreign Legion, crime (always from the detective's angle), the Great War (Air Force or Secret Service, not the infantry), the Tarzan motif in varying forms, professional football, tropical exploration, historical romance (Robin Hood, Cavaliers and Roundheads, etc.) and scientific invention. The Wild West still leads, at any rate as a setting, though the Red Indian seems to be fading out. The one theme that is really new is the scientific one. Death-rays, Martians, invisible men, robots, helicopters and inter-planetary rockets figure largely : here and there there are even far-off rumours of psychotherapy and ductless glands.'

This is from George Orwell's famous essay, 'Boys' Weeklies', written in 1939. He also observes that the new generation of weeklies he was describing—*Hotspur, Rover, Adventure* and the like—differed less than one might expect from those classic products of an earlier generation, *Magnet* and *Gem*. Since Orwell's essay was written, some of the weekly comics have died, some have been resurrected, many new ones have expired in infancy, and a few have enjoyed continuous unbroken life. The market is fiercely competitive, and some years ago it underwent a damaging crisis when the influence of American 'horror comics' provoked strong public reactions. Yet if one takes a representative collection of recent boys' comics and inspects their contents, one finds that Orwell's description is still broadly true —surprisingly little has changed.

The most striking change is the decline of the boys' school story. (Although the girls' weeklies, a newly abundant group

159

since Orwell's time, are dominated by stories set in schools: the difference is very interesting.) Apart from this, we have the mixture as before. The proportions have changed in predictable ways: the football story enjoys overwhelming ascendancy—a publication such as *Scorcher* accepts the existence of little else—and its only rival for popularity is the tale of the Second World War, which has naturally displaced the First. Crime is not a very conspicuous subject, but all the others in Orwell's list are still alive and ticking.

Not only are these aged themes still with us, but they are rarely threatened by anything new. When a weekly is seeking novelty its usual stratagem is to mix one favourite topic with another in some weird, outlandish way. A football team is trained by an African witch-doctor; an Allied agent in the Second World War acquires the power to store massive quantities of electricity within his person; a prehistoric caveman, having survived the passing centuries encased in ice, awakes to a lucrative career in boxing. Even those snippets of useless information are still there: 'The world record for throwing a 2 lb rolling pin is 135 ft 8 ins.' Perhaps a world which contains such oddities of fact can more credibly sustain its oddities of fiction; perhaps Redskin wrestlers really do survive plane crashes in the Australian outback. . . .

The cosy domesticity of comparable fare for girls is no surprise. The ponies are there, of course, and so are the chances to be nursemaid, and so are the tomboyish, excessively aquatic holidays. Football is naturally replaced by swimming, skating and athletics. School is at the centre. Not that the schools are always conspicuously normal. They tend to have a more than usually high proportion of teachers who are sinister foreign agents in search of plans, and a more than average proportion of girls whose fathers possess them. Alternatively, they can be rather genteel female versions of Dotheboys Hall. But where they exhibit such abnormalities, there is no shortage of resourceful girls at hand to bring things back to normal, where they rightly belong.

What attitudes should we take, as parents or teachers,

towards this prolific area of children's publishing? The problem would be eased if we could select some 'comics' and say with confidence that they were better than others, but in general this is not so. Not only are the contents monotonously similar, but the level of production is fairly uniform also. Most comics contain some strips in which the art-work is obviously good—crisp, vigorous and stylish, with the individual wit and strength of an accomplished cartoonist. Equally, most contain a good deal of drably unimaginative drawing, garish and insensitive colour-work, and weak story-lines. There is little to choose between one and another.

My own impression is that girls' comics are noticeably better than those for boys. The standard of printing and production, the art-work and the quality of the stories are all better, and the contents seem less single-mindedly 'escapist'. Not that escapism is necessarily a bad thing: more of that in a moment. But there are certain respects in which the material offered for girls is plainly more desirable than the boys' equivalent, and since the choice of material is usually determined by careful market research it is worth noting at least one difference which may reflect a small but important social trend. Orwell specified *professional* football as a major topic, and his qualification still holds true. The football stories largely concern major professional clubs, their star players and their star-bound young recruits; they emphasise the broad gap between the game watched and the game played, between the schoolboy's fierce loyalty to some large club, and his own practical experience as a player. They reflect, and must in turn encourage, the conversion of professional football into symbolic ritual, far removed from anything likely to involve the youngster as participant. He watches, and he worships, and the game he plays for fun is another matter entirely. Meanwhile the girls are getting busy. In their comics girls of their own age are swimming, or running, or doing gymnastics, and furthermore they are *training* to do these things, trying always to improve. One should not read too much into this, but the comics give a definite impression that the girls are lucky to have sports which are not as yet top-heavy with fame and success and overpraised achievement, so that their own role is not reduced to besotted spectatorship and improbable dreams of glory. If it is true, as some writers have suggested, that the wide circulation and sharp competition of the comics make them accurate reflectors of social mood, then the present mood as captured in the girls' weeklies is more vigorous and self-reliant, less dream-trapped than the boys'. But does it matter if the boys' comics are 'escapist'? This is one of the two essential questions we need to ask about comics, and not surprisingly it arouses sharp disagreements. Defenders of comics almost invariably maintain that the 'escapist' element is not merely harmless but positively desirable, offering a source of relief from the stresses and strains of daily living. People who take this view do not as a rule differentiate between 'comics' intended for adults and those published for children—adults and children alike, they argue, find in the slapstick comedy, or the fantastic adventure, or the dreamy wish-fulfilment, a pleasurable and necessary release from the limitations of ordinary life.

Many people profoundly disagree with this, though not always for the same reasons. It can be claimed (with some justice, if one selects the very worst examples) that comics are far from harmless, in that they frequently depict vicious cruelty as hilarious or thrilling. But even people who would accept that comics are 'harmless' would not necessarily excuse them on these grounds. What is 'harmless' may also be lifeless; instead of restoring our energies by affording short-term escape, the comics may weaken them by offering nothing but empty diversions. At their best the stories we read in childhood should give us the experience in fantasy of emotional crises we may come across in life, and help us to cope with them when they occur. The 'harmless' entertainment of the modern comic may have little help of this kind to offer, and its superficial attractions may actually reduce our ability to withstand the pressure of emotional upheaval. This, in brief, is the case for the prosecution.

At least one point of widespread agreement emerges, and my own inspection of the modern comic certainly confirms it. There

162

is very little in the comics which could cause shock or distress, and there is little danger that readers will be harmed by intrusions of the real and frightening. The reason for either defending or denouncing them is the opposite—that they are spiritless, anaemic compilations, characterised by empty sensationalism. They do not depict the real world, but replace it by some romanticised and comforting illusion. Nor do they offer true fantasy, for in true fantasy the pains of life can be faced and understood; instead they invest improbable events with a spurious realism which is immensely vivid but easily forgettable. They are set at just that point where a maximum of surface excitement is combined with a maximum of concealed inertia.

Does it matter? If a child's imaginative life is wholly or largely derived from the world of the comic, then in my view it does, because the quality of that imaginative life is enfeebled. On the other hand, a state of continuous emotional enrichment is not one that adults can sustain, and most of us read, or watch, or listen to something which we enjoy precisely because we know it is ephemeral and worthless, and so demands no effort. The 'inoffensiveness' of comics *can* be one of their virtues. Once again we have to think in terms of a balanced experience: as part of a larger pattern of reading, together with other sources of imaginative experience such as television and film, comics have a place. If they become more than that—more than a moderately active way of doing nothing whatever—it is perhaps time for parents to become concerned.

The second essential question which comics present us with concerns the relative importance of words and pictures. Here the defence of the comics is only one aspect of the defence of 'popular' arts in general. It hinges on the belief—one which is currently quite widespread—that the printed word has for many years carried excessive domination over the picture, and that the imbalance should and can be reversed. Because pictures have been so undervalued, the argument runs, they have split into two contrasting categories. Either they have been mere pulp for the uneducated (comics, 'lowbrow' films, etc.) or they have been the preserve of an intellectual élite (modern painting, 'highbrow' films, etc.). But now that printed material is more widely circulated than ever before, and the visual medium of television is generally available, increased exposure to pictures will cause the public to reject the dominant influence of printed language and turn to pictures instead. If one takes this view, the comics are only one item in a general and welcome cultural shift.

But there are many others who would admit that at present there is a marked trend towards pictures, but see it as a cause for alarm, not for approval. The reasons for resisting a pictorial revolution are many and various. So far as comics are concerned, opponents of this trend would certainly reject, for example, claims that comics stimulate a child's imagination or help him in learning to read.

The word or the picture?—that is the question. Obviously there are some places where the choice is unreal. The picture comics for very young children which depict the characters to be found in children's television programmes—programmes which are often of an extremely high standard—do a great deal of good. Similarly, a first-rate illustrator of children's fiction enriches the book he is illustrating, and is often an excellent writer himself. There is no encouragement to devalue the picture when one thinks of Edward Ardizzone, or Charles Keeping, or C Walter Hodges, or Antony Maitland. I think there is an answer to this question, but not a straightforward one.

The clue can be found in the work of such good illustrators as those I have just mentioned. If their work does not encourage the reader to devalue pictures, equally it does not encourage him to devalue words. They are not 'literary' artists in the bad sense—they are never slavishly providing a kind of photographic ornament to the printed text. But if they are not 'literary', they are certainly literate. Their pictures have an energy and substance of their own, but it is stimulated by the strength of their response to a story, and shows us how they have reacted to it. At its best their work is not only vivid illustration but vivid commentary on the story they are illustrating. Pictures like this can be dismissed as 'derivative', but they are no more derivative than any other work of art which is first germinated by a

Jack Holborn by Leon Garfield, illustrated by Antony Maitland

reaction to other artists. Virtually all art, in the widest sense, is 'derivative' in this kind of way, and none more so than Shakespeare's. What matters is that the artist's own enjoyment has generated something new, fresh and compelling—something which, in the case of an illustrator, may be closely attuned to a story, but also has its own virility and individualism. Antony Maitland's illustrations of Leon Garfield's novels are an excellent example of such work.

In some cases, the relationship between words and pictures is closer still—so close that we may be unable to disentangle the effect of one from the other. The younger the child, the more important the picture and the less important the word—of course. But even in stories for the youngest children there are pleasing rhymes and repetitions in the words which run in harness with the pleasures of familiar pictures. What this means is that from the beginning of a child's experience with books until the wider interests of adolescence there are rich possibilities for words and pictures to reinforce each other in a process of mutual enrichment. There are also opportunities throughout childhood for the pleasure of words by themselves, or pictures by themselves, and the pleasure will be greater if the storyteller has the gift of painting pictures in the mind, or the artist has a sense of narrative drive and movement. It is not necessary to claim that words are better than pictures, or vice versa.

It *is*, however, necessary to claim that experience of both is essential, and that the trend towards pictures and away from words may already have gone too far. It is doubtful whether pictures were ever so sharply divided into 'highbrow' and 'lowbrow' forms as some people have suggested, and doubtful also whether they were ever so dominated by the printed word. It is not an accident that the whole rich store of Christian literature has always been outweighed by the pictorial image of a man on a cross.

The danger we face nowadays is the reverse of word-monopoly. It is what has been accurately termed 'ever-increasing exposure to visual stimuli'. Comic-strips and comic-books are a part of this exposure, as are television, and film, and tabloid newspapers, and advertisement-hoardings, and colour supplements, and all the rest. One hopes that increased appreciation will accompany increased exposure, that the effects will be neither sensational nor anaesthetic. Only a continual process of education, together with an unstinted concern for quality in the visual stimuli themselves, can make sure of this. There is no need for the printed (or the spoken) word to be squeezed out, and the effect of television may be quite otherwise. (See Chapter 11.)

The circumstances which *could* have bad effects are these: a massive public which is content with easy, predigested visual entertainment, and an intellectual élite which scorns language and makes a cult out of selected types of picture, moving or still. The collapse of the printed word would be disastrous because it is inseparable from the deterioration of language itself, and language is able to make vastly more numerous, vastly finer and more delicate distinctions of meaning than is possible for any imaginable picture: it is the chief tool of civilisation, no less. Pictures are an older form of surviving self-expression for mankind—we can see what he drew before we can hear what he said. They can communicate with an intensity that language cannot match. They can cross national and racial frontiers with much greater ease. All this can be freely admitted, yet it remains true that when 'visual stimuli' begin to displace language men are beginning to sacrifice their power to exchange shades of meaning: they are stepping back.

And what has all this to do with a small child, prone on the hearthrug, reading *Beano*? Nothing, or much, depending on ourselves. If *Beano* is part of a whole environment of words and pictures, including much that is a great deal more demanding, we can welcome it. If it is part of our submission to a lifelong comic strip (perhaps without the balloons, sooner or later) then it is dangerous. Comics are 'good' or 'bad' for our children according to the world we build around them.

11 Television and Competing Media

In the 1930s a panic began in the United States when people took literally a dramatised version of H G Wells' *The War of the Worlds*, and believed that the earth had been invaded by Martians. In Great Britain, during the early years of expanded television services after the war, a thrilled and horrified audience watched Nigel Kneale's 'Quatermass' serials in a weekly ritual of terror. When *Quatermass and the Pit* was being shown, I was doing my postgraduate teaching practice in a boarding school, and I can still remember the solemn assembly which foregathered, congregation-like, in the masters' common room to face the compulsory weekly shudder.

These days, on the other hand, it is not the masters but the children who gather, not in the late evening but at Saturday teatime, to watch the BBC's *Doctor Who*. As I write, the latest episodes of this saga concern a piece of unidentified but voracious energy, a shapeless gobbler-up of living tissue, and the programme regularly exhibits items of mechanical or vegetable repulsiveness which make 'Quatermass' seem (as indeed it is) old hat.

What else is old hat, one wonders? Is fear old hat, is constraint old hat, is adult responsibility old hat? Something must be, or how can one account for the popularity of *Doctor Who*, and the cool enjoyment it provides for children whose parents were chilled to the marrow by far less horrifying things? The steel-nerved children who watch *Doctor Who* seem in little need of care and protection in their reading, or against any other stimuli that come their way.

Things are not quite so extreme, I think. If one forgets the programme itself for a moment and watches the children instead, it is usually clear that *Doctor Who* does not just thrill them. They find it funny, and are indeed invited to. The history of this programme is the story of something gradually finding its own level and its own ancestry, a feat it seems finally to have achieved. Beginning by taking itself much too seriously, it has gradually recognised the comic potential of horror, especially for its child audience: as a result, with every change of cast the central character of Doctor Who, while retaining his singular resourcefulness, has become more and more of a ridiculous crackpot.

In short, the programme is not an ingenious and compulsive time-fantasy at all; it is a cliché-ridden and farcical spine-chiller derived from the traditions of the comic. And like the best comic-strips (which have rightly kept their title even when most busily peddling horrors) it has increasingly poked fun at itself, and in doing so expanded its available repertoire of shocks and thrills. Laughter is the best antidote to fear.

For parents who worry about such things as *Doctor Who* there is a general point here which is worth remembering. Except in one important area, television and film have added very little that is new to the child's imaginative fare. As a rule they have borrowed a format or tradition which already existed in printed form, and transplanted it, with more or less success, to the screen. In spite of the fierce visual impact that some old-fashioned items have gained from the new media, there is little to suggest that they are actually taken more seriously. On the contrary, the norm seems to be that the small screen makes them funnier than they were, or gives them a strange engaging domesticity. Perhaps the most striking example of this is the nationwide affection inspired by Doctor Who's enemies, the Daleks, even at the time when the programme was trying really hard to be frightening. In miniature, the history of this series is a good example of two pronounced tendencies of television: its capacity to neutralise horror, which for its adult audience is not an unmixed blessing, and its capacity to create superb comedy.

The exception to television's largely derivative nature lies in the programmes for infants and young children. It is not necessary to say much about them—loud applause will do well enough. The BBC's 'Magic Roundabout' series is a really outstanding example of continuous, sustained excellence in a field of broadcasting where we have almost come to take high standards for granted. For anyone who already has, it is worth stressing that the contribution made by television to the imaginative life of the under-fives is not much short of revolutionary. Over and over again, in series after series, the television channels have achieved a warm, uninsistent intimacy of story-telling and shared pleasure, and demonstrated a capacity for contact which is felt by the child to be direct and personal —extraordinary successes in a medium which has a habit of staying persistently cold. The same high standard is kept up for children a year or two older in *Jackanory*, where good stories are all the better for good telling, and the temptations to over-dramatise are rightly resisted.

If most programmes are somehow derived from more familiar media, these highly original creations for the very young habitually lead back towards them. The most popular figures in these series re-appear in 'comics' for the pre-school child, and in little books, and sundry other guises. With the initial stimulus of the programmes behind them, they form links with the world of books and contribute to the young child's wider pleasure in pictures and words. Even at this level, where television is at its most inventive and distinguished, a two-way process is going on which transmits the successes of one medium into the world of another, and there is little doubt that the best of television for the young has a strong and positive effect in creating a readiness to gain pleasure from looking at books, or reading and listening to stories at home. To see the television set as somehow being in competition with other (more 'cultural') activities such as looking at picture-books is mistaken. The activities are not so different as they seem, and have plenty of educative pleasures in common —they refresh and reinforce each other, combining to produce small children with lively imaginations, well-stocked minds and high expectations, who will go to school with plenty to talk about. And if it seems a wearisome truism that children *always* have plenty to talk about, that is only because we have come to take enriching infancy for granted.

Television for the older child may not arouse quite such strong enthusiasm. Young viewers have ready access to endless stores of imbecile rubbish designed to alleviate adult boredom: *Crossroads* perhaps deserves the award of the Golden Yawn for the most spacious emptiness available. But the same point is true of television, and of films, as of books: we cannot complain on behalf of our children at the low quality of mass-material supplied for ourselves, to meet our own demands. Almost invariably, when the television channels produce material with young viewers specifically in mind, they do so with admirable intelligence and responsibility, even if the actual results do not always match the aspiration.

There are, for example, occasional serialisations of books for young readers, and in the last year or two these have included John Rowe Townsend's *The Intruder* and Alan Garner's *The Owl Service*. The actual merits of the television versions are open to dispute: both are books of high quality and considerable imaginative strength, but they did not for that reason seem immune to the small screen's gifts for unintended humour. What is also striking about such adaptations is their tendency to fail on just those matters where they ought possibly to improve on the book—in the vivid realisation of landscapes and settings, for example. The bleak, decaying shorescape of *The Intruder* ought to have a powerful atmospheric effect on the screen, but the actual results were more suggestive of a fifth-rate resort out of season than of the depopulated and treacherous wilderness in Townsend's novel. As a piece of scene-painting his own words were considerably more impressive than anything the camera achieved, and the wider suggestiveness, the intensely poetic significance assumed by the landscape in his book was entirely missing. Serious and well-intentioned filming does not by any means ensure that a powerful book for young readers can be translated effectively into the continuous pictorial imagery of television or film—the production problems are major ones.

The fate of the book itself, however, once it has been shown on television, is altogether less hazardous. There is a virtually foolproof guarantee that it will be widely read, and the prompt appearance in the bookshops of numerous paperback copies is pretty well assured! In the case of *The Owl Service*, it was possible to buy not only a paperback of the novel itself but another recounting the whole process of television filming. Once again there is plainly a two-way process, by which television, which may certainly occupy some time which would otherwise be spent in reading, also stimulates and encourages reading by the interest and excitement which its serials, in particular, generate.

The reason why a televised book usually becomes so popular is not entirely easy to determine. Part of the attraction is undoubtedly that of retracing a story which one already knows, and bears comparison with the pleasures of re-reading—pleasures which young children are seeking when they demand endless repetitions of the same tale, and which continue to satisfy us to a lesser extent almost indefinitely. On the other hand one might expect that the documentary thoroughness of television production, which supplies well-defined images and leaves little scope for imagination, would exhaust the possibilities of a book more quickly than a reading, and leave one feeling that nothing further need be said. What really happens seems to be the reverse of this. Television, with its intensity of focus, pace and concentration, can be most effective dramatically and yet leave a penumbra of doubt and mystery—a feeling that there is more to be had, interests beyond the edges of the screen, which lead one in search of answers from the book.

When television adapts the classics, there is of course no question that this extra dimension exists. No televised version can render an adequate visual and dramatic equivalent of a great novel, although it can use the resources of its own medium to capture the narrative qualities which particularly call for pictorial expression. The most successful television adaptations are the adventurous ones, which do not attempt a slavish fidelity to the original, but alter the weight and emphasis to suit the new medium. Here again the effect of television is to stimulate reading of the original. No doubt there is a high failure rate in consequence—books purchased in hope and abandoned in disappointment—but this is only to be expected, and needs to be set against the mass of reading pleasure which would not have otherwise occurred. The same point applies to the filming of books like *The Owl Service* and *The Intruder*, except that here the failure rate is likely to be appreciably lower.

The cinema can do equally good service. A typical example of its effects was the film of E Nesbit's *The Railway Children*, a so-called 'family film' which roused some critical disapproval and enormous popular success. The story was undeniably romanticised by the film—clean and charming engines chugged happily through a too-green countryside, and the book's faith in the kindliness of human nature was perhaps too heavily endorsed. Such a film can be too self-consciously entertaining, and flash its happy messages without the reserve and qualification of the original story. For something so straightforwardly delightful as this film, the price is a small one to pay: what mattered was the obvious enjoyment of those who *made* the film, as well as those who saw it, and the enjoyment on both sides sprang from everyone's unembarrassed pleasure in a period-piece. As a modern film, its integrity depended on accepting this, and keeping a proper balance between the modern medium and modern attitudes of its makers, and the timeless medium but bygone attitudes of the original novel.

This kind of integrity—integrity to the chosen medium itself, and to changes in values and attitudes where these exist—is intrinsic to successful interaction between books and other media. In film and television there is obviously much to disapprove of, and a great deal more which is simply nondescript and ephemeral. The same is true of books, and magazines, and papers. But the fears of a few years ago, that the eye in the sitting-room corner would eventually outstare all reading and cultivate a universal mindlessness, does not seem in the least supported by events. It is the fantasy on which Ray Bradbury's story, *Fahrenheit 451*, is based, and it remains a fantasy, with

173

none of the disturbing tendencies of another futuristic novel, Huxley's *Brave New World*, to convert itself into everyday truth. Instead the signs are that positive and beneficial interactions can occur, and that one medium or art-form has the power to support and enrich another. It is important to recognise the things which books can do and film or television cannot— there really is no substitute for the permanent written word. But it is just as important not to belittle the quality of pleasure which film and television have brought to the lives of modern children. The media are not in competition unless we, as parents and teachers, permit them to be, by neglecting our responsibility to make rich experiences widely and freely available, in *all* the media we are lucky enough to command.

12 Slow, Backward or Reluctant?

A note of advice on children with reading difficulties.

This book is mainly intended for parents and teachers working with children of 'normal' reading development, and I have emphasised the enormous variety of standards and choices that 'normality' can properly include: the fact that a child persistently chooses books which are 'too young' for him is *not* in itself a sign of 'backwardness'.

The problem of the 'backward' or 'reluctant' reader is a very complex one, and I have not thought it right to over-simplify it by attempting some sketchy answer in a book which is mainly concerned with other things. This is not because I underestimate the importance of the problem or the anxiety it can cause to parents, but because I would wish to *insist* on its importance and its 'specialist' nature. This note is therefore intended not to supply answers but to give directions for further enquiry.

The first essential is to identify the problem, and for that one must distinguish clearly between terms which are often used interchangeably. The slow reader should be termed 'backward' if he experiences difficulty in mastering the physical act of reading and if his 'reading age' falls seriously in arrears of his actual age. He should be termed 'reluctant' if he is quite capable of reading but is not interested in doing so. If a child has a 'reading problem' it is vital to determine which category it belongs to.

Parents who wish to understand their child's problem should

obviously consult the teacher, who can advise them what kind of help to give. I would also strongly recommend three books:

> *The Slow Reader* by R C Ablewhite (Heinemann)
>
> *The Reluctant Reader* by Aidan Chambers (Pergamon Press)
>
> *Reading—which approach?* by Vera Southgate and Geoffrey R Roberts (University of London Press).

These are not suggested as alternatives: they cover different aspects of the problem. *The Slow Reader* deals lucidly with technical questions of learning to read, and distinguishes very helpfully between the reading problems of the young child and those of the adolescent. *The Reluctant Reader* deals with the problem of stimulating interest in those who are not attracted by reading, and contains much useful comment on particular books. *Reading—which approach?* is a survey of the main methods now used in teaching reading, and may help anxious parents to understand what the school is doing and why it is not doing something else. All three books are as free of obstructive jargon as one could fairly hope for.

Parents are often chary of consulting the teacher, but there are occasions when it is essential to do so. Schools should welcome such contact, not regard it as a nuisance, but any parent who finds that he is being treated as a nuisance on such matters should press on regardless and attempt to be the most polite, and the most implacable nuisance that the school has ever met. Three such essential occasions are these:

i) If a child has a 'reading problem' which the school is treating, no parent should ever attempt any amateur supplementary 'teaching' unless it has the school's knowledge and consent. Otherwise it may be accidentally damaging to work which the school is doing. Obviously it is desirable for parents to follow up and support the school's work if they usefully can, and obviously they cannot do so without consulting the teachers in the first place.

ii) If a parent has any reason to suppose that a 'reading problem' may be due to an undetected (and possibly trivial)

176

medical condition, he should not hesitate to press for specialist examination. In this case it would be natural to seek advice first of all from the child's own doctor.

iii)   If a child changes schools (and this applies just as much to the child who is learning to read in the normal way as to the one receiving remedial teaching) this may involve a change of teaching method. Parents cannot insist that a child should continue with a system he has already started: for a primary school the choice of a reading scheme involves a considerable investment, and it would be impossible (on grounds of cost, administration, and teaching expertise) for a school to carry a kind of 'spare parts' service for children previously taught by a different method. What parents can and should insist on is that the receiving teacher *knows* what method was previously used, *and arranges an effective process of transition* from the one to the other. In theory this problem would be covered by inter-school communication. In practice the parent had better make sure. No child, either at the initial learning or the remedial stage, should be abruptly transferred from one system to another.

For further advice on these and related matters affecting relations between the parent and the school, the following are strongly recommended:

> *Home and School* by Tyrrell Burgess (Allen Lane the Penguin Press)
>
> *Where/On Parents and Law* (Advisory Centre for Education, 32 Trumpington Street, Cambridge).

Apart from such complications, however, the best course for parents is essentially the same as that which I have advocated throughout the book: the provision of a home environment in which books are available, reading is seen to be valued and practised, children are read to if they enjoy it, and are encouraged to expect, and to search for, independent pleasure in reading. To conclude with, here is a list of some useful series which are aimed specifically at the 'backward' or the 'reluctant' reader: those for adolescents usually have story-lines likely to interest teenagers, but a style and vocabulary appropriate to

177

younger children. In some cases the books are published with one age group in mind, but are suitable for older readers with a reading difficulty. They are listed in ascending order of demand (approximately), beginning with 'backward' readers amongst older juniors and ending with 'reluctant' adolescents:

'I Can Read' Books	World's Work
Beginner Books	Collins
'Windrush' Books	Oxford
'Bandit' Books	Benn
'Tempo' Books	Kestrel
'Focus' Books	Blackie
'Hurricane' Books	Chatto and Windus
'Dolphin' Books	University of London Press
'Trend' Books	(distributed by Ginn)
'Inner Ring' Books	Benn
Rescue Reading	Ginn
'Jets' Books	Cape
'Joan Tate Books'	Heinemann
'Topliners'	Macmillan
'Pyramid Books'	Heinemann

In some cases the catalogue price of these series is based on bulk purchase by schools; you may have to pay a little extra if you order an individual copy through a bookseller.

13 Further Information

Organisations

1 *The Federation of Children's Book Groups* (Secretary: Mrs Clodagh Alborough, 27 High Street, Owston Ferry, Doncaster, Yorks).

For parents this is much the most constructive development of the last few years; its purpose is to bring together interested parents in particular areas to conduct a wide range of activities designed to promote understanding of the importance of children's literature. These activities include organising exhibitions, arranging for talks by authors and critics, catering for the needs of areas not served by good bookshops, and exchanging information as effectively as possible. Details of existing groups, and advice on forming new ones, are available from the Secretary at the above address.

2 *The National Book League* (7 Albemarle Street, London, W1X 4BB; 1121 Paisley Road West, Glasgow, SW2).

The League gives special attention to children's books, issuing regular catalogues and book-lists, holding exhibitions, providing—through the Reference Collection of Current Children's Books—guidance on recent publications, and supplying many other useful services.

3 *The Advisory Centre for Education* (32 Trumpington Street, Cambridge, CB2 1QY).

ACE is generally concerned with establishing closer links between parents and teachers, home and school, and with promoting parents' influence over their children's education. Its magazine *Where* frequently contains useful articles concerned with reading.

Journals containing reviews

a   Newspapers

Regular reviews of children's books are to be found only in *The Times*, *The Guardian*, *The Sunday Times*, and *The Observer*, and of these it is *The Guardian* which provides the freshest and most helpful reviewing. *The Times Literary Supplement* and *The Times Educational Supplement* each issue children's book sections three times a year, and the British Council's *British Book News* now reviews children's books regularly. Otherwise most newspapers and periodicals only review children's books at Christmas and Easter, and even on these rare occasions their notices are often too perfunctory to be very much use. The same, regrettably, applies to radio and television.

b   Specialist journals

If you can afford it, the best way of keeping up to date is to subscribe to at least one of the regular specialist journals. Two which offer the greatest help to parents are:

Books for your Children (edited by Anne Wood, founder of the Federation of Children's Book Groups). 4 issues per year, from 14 Stoke Road, Guildford, Surrey.

Growing Point (edited by Margery Fisher, author of *Intent Upon Reading* and *Matters of Fact*). 9 issues per year, from Ashton Manor, Northampton.

Also strongly recommended:

Signal: approaches to children's books. 3 issues a year, from the Thimble Press, Stroud, Glos. GL5 5BA.

Children's Book Review. 6 issues a year, from Five Owls Press Ltd., 67 High Road, Wormley, Broxbourne, Herts.

Junior Bookshelf. 6 issues a year, from Marsh Hall, Thurstonland, Huddersfield, Yorkshire.

The School Librarian. School Library Association, 150 Southampton Row, London WC1.

Books

From a gradually increasing range of books available—some of which are rather too specifically aimed at teachers, and tending perhaps to invent a specialist expertise from which parents are excluded—the following can be specially recommended for further reading :

Children's Books of the Year (Hamish Hamilton, in association with the British Council and the National Book League). Intended as an annual series of guides to publications for children in the course of a year.

Intent Upon Reading by Margery Fisher (Brockhampton). Mrs Fisher's contribution to informed interest in children's books can hardly be overestimated, and *Intent Upon Reading* is an important book. She is an over-tolerant critic, perhaps, but a wise one.

Matters of Fact by Margery Fisher (Brockhampton). A more recent companion-volume to *Intent Upon Reading*. It is exclusively concerned with non-fiction, and may therefore be of special interest to readers looking for help in areas not covered in this book.

A Sense of Story by John Rowe Townsend (Kestrel). Studies of the work of nineteen modern authors, followed by comments from the writers themselves. Readers may find it a particularly interesting follow-up to this book.

The Nesbit Tradition: The Children's Novel in England 1945–70 by Marcus Crouch (Benn). Rather too much like a densely-populated catalogue, but it includes many incisive critical judgements, some of which differ markedly from mine.

Children Are People by Janet Hill (Hamish Hamilton). A vigorous account of imaginative children's librarianship, of much interest to parents and teachers. See also *Children's Libraries* by Ann Fleet (Deutsch).

British Children's Books in the Twentieth Century by Frank Eyre (Kestrel).

A number of brief, perceptive essays on individual authors can also be found in 'Bodley Head Monographs', edited by Kathleen Lines.

Index

Ablewhite, R C, 176
Abridgement, 118–119
Adams, Richard, 147
Adamson, Gareth, 56, 66
Adamson, George, 53
Adamson, Jean, 56
Adolescent reading, 22, 23, 135–150 ,176–178
Aiken, Joan, 75, 105–108, 113
Alcott, Louisa M, 133
Alice in Wonderland, 122, 124, 126
Alice Through the Looking Glass, 125
Allan, Mabel Esther, 150
Allingham, Margery, 135
Allsop, Kenneth, 15
Almedingen, E M, 146
Ambrus, Victor G, 56
Andersen, Hans, 132
Annotated Alice, The, 118
Antelope Books, 63
Ardizzone, Aingelda, 71
Ardizzone, Edward, 55, 56, 71, 129, 132, 164
Armada Books, 38
Arnold, Elliott, 148
Arthur, Ruth, 149
Arundel, Honor, 149, 150
As You Like It, 15
Ash Road, 86–88
Avery, Gillian, 72, 87, 112
Awdry, Rev. W, 55

Baker, Margaret J, 150
Balderson, Margaret, 91
Ballantyne, R M, 128, 133
Ballard, Martin, 150
Banbery, Fred, 56
Bandit Books, 178
Bateman, Robert, 90

Baumann, Hans, 56, 110, 146
Bawden, Nina, 75 91
Baxter, Gillian, 75
Baylor, Byrd, 73
'BB', 14–15, 61, 63, 73–4, 91
Beano, 167
Beckett, Samuel, 125
Beginner Books, 178
Beresford, Elisabeth, 55
Berna, Paul, 93
Bevis, 122
Bible, 120, 121, 129–30
Bicknell, Sally, 150
'Biggles' books, 18, 24
'Black Banner' series, 136
Black Banner Abroad, 136–137
Black Hearts in Battersea, 107–108
Blackmore, R D, 134
Blake, Quentin, 56
Blake, William, 61
Blakeley, Peggy, 53
Blish, James, 114
Blishen, Edward, 95, 130
Blyton, Enid, 17, 30, 31, 32, 33, 153–158
Bond, James, 21
Bond, Michael, 33, 56, 59–60, 73
Bond, Ruskin, 72
Books for New Adults, 150
Boothroyd, Basil, 101
Borchers, Elizabeth, 72
'Borrowers', The', 63, 74
Bosco, Henri, 92
Boston, Lucy M, 75, 102, 112
Boswell, Hilda, 54
Boucher, Alan, 131
Bows Against the Barons, 99
'Boys' Weeklies', 159
Bradbury, Ray, 173–174

Branfield, John, 148
Brave New World, 174
Breck, Vivian, 150
Brendon Chase, 14
Brennan, Nicholas, 56
Briggs, Raymond, 54, 72
Brinsmead, H F, 92–3, 150
Brontë, Charlotte, 133
Brown, Michael, 129
Brown on Resolution, 15
Brown, Roy, 71, 75, 82, 92, 93
Bruna, Dick, 53, 54, 55
Brunhoff, Jean de, 54
Burgess, Tyrrell, 177
Burnett, Frances Hodgson, 70, 132
Burningham, John, 53
Burton, Hester, 91, 112, 146
Butts, Dennis, 17, 18
Byars, Betsy, 75

Carnegie Medal, 14, 64, 89, 95, 130
'Carousel' books, 38
Carpelan, Bo, 149
Carroll, Lewis, 122–126, 132
Carroll, Ruth, 53
Cary, Joyce, 23, 149
Cathedral Wednesday, 156
Cawley, Winifred, 146
Chambers, Aidan, 176
Chance, Stephen, 150
Chaney, Jill, 149
Chapman, Gaynor, 131
Charley is my Darling, 23
Chauncy, Nan, 92
Child-Buyer, The, 81
Children of the New Forest, The, 127
'Choice of Paperbacks, A' 101
Choristers' Cake, 155

Christopher, John, 101, 114
Chrysalids, The, 100, 101
Church, Richard, 113
Clark, Mavis Thorpe, 93
Clarke, Arthur C, 114
Clarke, Pauline, 131
Cleaver, Vera and Bill, 149
Clewes, Dorothy, 73, 93
Cole, Michael and Joanne, 57
Colwell, Eileen, 55
Conan Doyle, Sir Arthur, 33
Connor, Chris, 130
Conrad, Joseph, 15, 84
Cookson, Catherine, 91, 112
Coolidge, Susan, 32, 133
Cooper, Susan, 113
Coral Island, The, 122, 128
Cordell, Alexander, 148
Corrin, Sara and Stephen, 55, 71, 72
Country Child, The, 103
Couper, J M, 148, 150
Crane, Stephen, 133
Cresswell, Helen, 54, 59, 66–68, 70, 71, 73, 74
Crossley-Holland, Kevin, 111, 121, 131
'Crossroads', 171
Cue for Treason, 32
Cummings, Primrose, 28, 91
Curry, Jane Louise, 112, 113

Darke, Marjorie, 112
David Copperfield, 107
Dawn Wind, 98
Defoe, Daniel, 133
Derwent, Lavinia, 130
Devil's Children, The, 100
Dickens, Charles, 42, 126–127, 133
Dickinson, Peter, 91, 100–102, 112, 114, 120
Didacticism, 24, 25, 32
Dillon, Eilis, 72, 75, 91
'Doctor Who', 168–169
Dolphin books, 178
Druce, Robert, 113
Drummer Boy, The, 96–97
Drummond, V H, 56

Eagle of the Ninth, The, 98
Edwards, Dorothy, 55
Edwards, Monica, 113

Elidor, 113
Estes, Eleanor, 73
Evans, C S, 55

Fahrenheit 451, 173–174
Fairfax-Lucy, Brian, 150
Fairy tales, 22, 51, 120
Falkner, J Meade, 134
'Famous Five' series, 153
Fantasy, 22, 77, 94, 100–109, 141–144, 162, 163, 173
Farjeon, Eleanor, 72, 128
Farmer, Penelope, 33, 112, 130
Farrar, F W, 133
Farthest Shore, The, 144
Films, 15, 17, 119, 163, 164, 166, 169, 171, 173, 174
Finn's Folly, 23, 88–89
Firmin, Peter, 55
Fisher, Margery, 72
Fisk, Nicholas, 93, 113
Flambards, 137–141, 142
Flanders, Michael, 129
Fleming, Ian, 21
Flowers of Adonis, The, 99
Fly-by-Night, 28
Focus Books, 178
Forest, Antonia, 90, 111
Forest of Boland Light Railway, The, 14
Forester, C S, 15
Four Rode Home, 28
Freeman, Don, 56
Frewer, Glyn, 112
Fromm, Lilo, 54
Future Took Us, The, 102
Futuristic books, 100–102, 173, 174
Fyson, J G, 110

Gallico, Paul, 33
Garfield, Leon, 32, 75, 94, 95, 96–97, 98, 112, 113, 130, 147, 166
Garner, Alan, 33, 64, 113, 141–143, 147, 171–172, 173
'Gazelle Books', 63
Gem, 159
George, Jean, 91
Gilman, Robert, 147
Glanville, Brian, 90
God Beneath The Sea, The, 95
Goldie, Fay, 146
Golding, William, 15, 19, 100, 128

Goodall, John S, 54
Gordon, John, 113, 143, 147
Gordon, Richard, 33
Goudge, Elizabeth, 33, 73, 113
Grahame, Kenneth, 39, 133
Graveston, Mary, 147
Gray, Nicholas Stuart, 113
Great Expectations, 120
'Green Knowe' series, 102
Green, Roger Lancelyn, 121, 130, 131
Greene, Graham, 13–14, 19, 50, 71
Gretz, Susanna, 53
Grice, Frederick, 75, 92
Grimm, the Brothers, 132
Grimshaw, Nigel, 75
Gudmundson, J Shirley, 93
Guillot, Rene, 33, 74
Guin, Ursula le, 114, 144, 147
Gulliver's Travels, 119, 122, 125–126
Gumble's Yard, 33, 127

Hadfield, Alice M, 131
Haggard, H Rider, 134
Halliwell, James Orchard, 54
Hamley, Dennis 112
Hardcastle, Michael, 75, 90, 150
Harnett, Cynthia, 94–96, 97, 98, 111
Harris, Mary, 90
Harris, Rosemary, 121, 130, 143–144, 149
Haviland, Virginia, 54
Hay, Dean, 53
Heartsease, 100–101
Heinlein, Robert A, 147
Herrmann, Reinhard, 54, 129
Hersey, John, 81
Historical fiction, 94–99, 101–102
Hoban, Russell, 39, 56, 73, 113
Hobbit, The, 126
Hodges, C Walter, 111, 129, 164
Hollowood, Jane, 72
Home and School, 177
Hope-Simpson, Jacynth, 93, 129

Horse and his Boy, The, 66
Horsemen on the Hills, 99
Hotspur, 159
Hough, Charlotte, 73
House on the Brink, The, 143
Household, Geoffrey, 18
Howell, Margaret, 72
Huddy, Delia, 71
Hughes, Shirley, 57
Hughes, Ted, 73
Hughes, Thomas, 133
Hull, Katharine, 91
Hunter, Evan, 21
Hunter, Mollie, 66–67, 74, 110, 150
Hurricane books, 178
Hutchins, Pat, 38, 46–48, 54, 56
Huxley, Aldous, 174

'I Can Read' books, 178
Illustration, 43–49, 119, 161, 163, 164, 166–177
'Inner Ring' books, 178
Innes, Michael, 109
Intruder, The, 33, 171, 173
Ireson, Barbara, 55

Jack Holborn, 97
'Jackanory', 170
Jane Eyre, 117, 122
Jansson, Tove, 72
Jefferies, Richard, 133
'Jets' books, 178
'Joan Tate' books, 178
Johns, Captain, W E, 19
Jones, Howard, 111
Jong, Meindert de, 75
Josh, 89
Journeying Boy, The, 109

Kamm, Josephine, 130, 148
Kasuya, Masahiro, 54
Keeping, Charles, 45–46, 48, 57, 130, 164
Keith, Harold, 147
Kelpie's Pearls, The, 67
Kim, 24
King, Clive, 75, 113
King Lear, 105
Kingsley, Charles, 133
Kipling, Rudyard, 39, 133, 134
'Kiss Me, Dudley', 21
Kitt, Tamara, 72
Kneale, Nigel, 168
'Knight' books, 38
Knights of Bushido, The, 20

Krahn, Fernando, 53–54
Kroll, Edite, 148

'Ladybird' books, 50
Lang, Andrew, 130
Lantern Bearers, The, 39, 95
Last Battle, The, 64–66
Legend, 120, 121, 129, 141–144
l'Engle, Madeleine, 73, 113
Lester, Julius, 25, 75, 149
Lewis, C S, 64–66, 74
Lewis, Hilda, 111
Libne (Lieberman), Zvi, 146
Libraries, 26–28, 153
Line, David, 92
Lines, Kathleen, 71, 130
Lingard, Joan, 147
'Listen With Mother', 55
Little Grey Men, The, 14, 61
Little Women, 117, 122, 127
Lively, Penelope, 112, 113
Lord, Beman, 53
Lord of the Flies, 15, 100, 128
Lord of the Rings, The, 126
Lore and Language of Schoolchildren, The, 118–119
Lost Childhood and Other Essays, The, 51

Macbeth, 118
Macbeth, George, 129
McCallum, Graham, 130
Macdonald, George, 129, 133
Maclean, Alistair, 135
McLean, Allan Campbell, 93
McLeish. Kenneth, 56
McNeill, Janet, 70, 72
'Magic Roundabout', 50, 170
Magician's Nephew, The, 66
Magnet, 159
Mahy, Margaret, 73
Maitland, Antony, 73, 164, 166
Makhanlall, David P, 75
Marchand, Jacques le, 130
Mare, Walter de la, 133
Mari, Iela, 54

Mark of the Horse Lord, The, 99
Marks, J M, 147
Marryat, Captain, 133
Marsh, Gwen, 73
Masefield, John, 113
Mattingly. Christobel, 71
Maxwell, Gavin, 33
Mayne, William, 155–157
Meyer, Renate, 53, 73
Milne, A A, 33, 39, 51, 57, 59–60, 126
Missee Lee, 83
Moby Dick, 107
Monsarrat, Nicholas, 18
Montgomerie, Norah, 55
Montgomery, L M, 133
'Moominland' books, 72
Moon in the Cloud, The, 121
Moon of Gomrath, The, 113
Morgan, Helen, 60–61, 73
Mouse and His Child, The, 113
Mrs Pinny and the Blowing Day, 60–61
Murphy, 125
'My Naughty Little Sister' stories, 33, 51
Myths, 22, 95, 120, 129

'Narnia', 64–65, 74
Naughton, Bill, 90
Nesbit, E, 70, 129, 132, 173
Newby, P H, 148
Night Birds on Nantucket, 105, 107
Night-Watchmen, The, 68, 70
Nineteenth Century Children, 87
Norton, André, 73, 114, 147
Norton, Mary, 63, 74
Nostromo, 15
Nourse, Alan E, 114
Nursery rhymes, 16, 22, 118, 120, 125
'Nutshell Library', 53
Nye, Robert, 131

Oakley, Graham, 56
O'Dell, Scott, 150
Oman, Carola, 131
Once and Future King, The, 120
Opie, Iona and Peter, 54, 118–119

Orwell, George, 159–160, 161
Outcast, 22
Owl Service, The, 141–143, 171–172, 173
Overton, Jenny, 75, 93
Oxenbury, Helen, 53, 132

'Paddington' series, 59–60, 72
Palmer, C Everard, 93
Paperbacks 38
Parker, Richard, 75, 92, 112
Parkinson, C Northcote, 91
Patrick Kentigern Keenan, 66–67
'Peacock' books, 150
Peake, Mervyn, 132
Pearce, Philippa, 73, 75, 91, 103–105, 112, 150
Pennington's Seventeenth Summer, 23
Peppé, Rodney, 53
Peyton, K M, 23, 28, 33, 91, 112, 137–141, 148
Piatti, Celestino, 53, 71
Piatti, Ursula 71
Picard, Barbara Leonie, 131
'Piccolo' books, 38
Plowman, Stephanie, 146, 147
'Pooh' books, 51, 59–60
Poole, Josephine, 113
Pope, Ray, 150
Porter, Sheena, 92
Postgate, Oliver, 55, 71
Potter, Beatrix, 50–51, 54, 57, 61, 71, 126
Potter, Margaret, 93
Power, Rhoda, 110
Prester John, 24
Pride and Prejudice, 117
Prince, Alison, 57, 71
Prince in Waiting, The, 101
Proctor, David, 147
Pyle, Howard, 131
'Pyramid' books, 150, 178

'Quatermass and the Pit', 168

Railway Children, The, 70, 127, 173
Ransome, Arthur, 82–84, 93
Ravensgill, 156

Reading—which approach?, 176
Reed, Talbot Baines, 134
Reeves, James, 56, 129, 130, 131, 132, 133
Reid, Meta Mayne, 112
Reluctant Reader, The, 176
Renault, Mary, 130
'Rescue Reading,' 178
Re-writing, 119–122
Rey, Lester del, 147
Richards, Frank, 32
Richter, Hans Peter, 148
Roberts, Geoffrey R, 176
Robinson Crusoe, 122, 127
Robinson, Joan G, 91, 102, 112, 149
Robinson, Veronica, 92
Roland, Betty, 73
Rose, Elizabeth and Gerald, 54
Rosie's Walk, 38, 46–48
Ross, Diana, 55
Roth, David, 92
Rover, 159
Russell of Liverpool, Lord, 20–21
Ryan, John, 55

Salinger, J D, 149
Salkey, Andrew, 93
'Sam Pig' books, 61
Saville, Malcolm, 33, 149
Scorcher, 160
Scott, Sir Walter, 133
Scourge of the Swastika, The, 20
Sea Mice, The, 115–116
Sea-Thing Child, The, 39
Seal-Singing, The, 143–144
Secret Garden, The, 70
Secret Places and Other Essays, 51
'Secret Seven' series, 153
Seed, Jenny, 75
Sendak, Maurice, 38, 43–46, 48, 53, 57, 58, 59, 73
Serraillier, Ian, 91, 93, 121, 127, 130, 131
Seuss, Dr, 53, 56
Severn, David, 102, 112
Sewell, Anna, 133
Shadow Line, The, 84
Shakespeare, William, 15, 19, 32, 51, 105, 166
Shardlow, Paul, 54
Sherry, Silvia, 92
Shub, Elizabeth, 132
Shute, Nevil, 135

Signposters, The, 68
Silver Chair, The, 66
Silver Flame, 15
Silver Sword, The, 32, 127
Simon, 99
Sleigh, Barbara, 54
Slow Reader, The, 176
Smith, Emma, 72, 92
Smith, Vian, 75, 150
Softly, Barbara, 56
Southall, Ivan, 84–89, 92–3, 129, 150, 156
Southgate, Vera, 176
Speare, Elizabeth George, 110
Sperry, Armstrong, 74
Spillane, Micky, 21
Steel, David, 101
Steele, Mary Q, 113
Steinbeck, John, 33
Stevenson, R L, 133
Stewart, Mary, 135
Stewart, Morna, 110
Storey, Margaret, 92, 149
Storr, Catherine, 93, 113
'Storychair Books', 38
Streatfeild, Noel, 33, 70, 91
Sudbery, Rodie, 93
Suddaby, Donald, 131
Sutcliff, Rosemary, 22, 32, 33, 39, 72, 74, 94, 95, 97–99, 111, 121, 131, 146
Swallows and Amazons, 82–83
Swallowdale, 83
Swarm in May, A, 156
Swift, Jonathan, 125–126, 133
Swiss Family Robinson, The, 122, 127
Sword at Sunset, 99
Sykes, Pamela, 112
Symons, Geraldine, 150

Television, 15, 16, 17, 22, 119, 163, 164, 166, 167, 166, 167, 168–174
Tempest, The, 15
'Tempo' books, 178
Thomas, Dylan, 60, 61
Thomas, Gwyn, 61
Thompson, Eric, 55
Through the Window, 45–46, 48
To Be a Slave, 25
To Kill a Mocking Bird, 33
Todd, Barbara Euphan, 72

Tolkien, J R R, 33, 113, 126
Tom and Sam, 48
Tom Brown's Schooldays, 115–116, 117, 122
Tom's Midnight Garden, 103–105
Tom Sawyer, 77–82, 84, 87, 108
'Tom Sawyer—Delinquent', 81
Tomalin, Ruth, 75, 93, 115–116, 149
Tombs of Atuan, The, 144
'Topliners', 150, 178
Townsend, John Rowe, 33, 75, 92, 127, 149, 171
Translations, 121
Traveller in Time, A, 102–103
Treadgold, Mary, 28, 90, 91
Trease, Geoffrey, 75, 90, 99, 110, 111, 131, 136–137, 138, 146, 149
Treasure Island, 117, 122, 127
Treece, Henry, 32, 92, 110, 131
'Trend' books, 178
Trevino, Elizabeth Borton de, 110
Trilling, Diana, 81
Tucker, Nicholas, 55
Turner, Philip, 92, 112
Twain, Mark, 77–82, 133, 150

Under Milk Wood, 60
Unsworth, Walter, 112
Use of English, The, 17, 155

Uttley, Alison, 51, 61, 71, 102–103, 112

Verne, Jules, 33, 134
Victory, 15
Vipont, Elfrida, 70, 90
Voyage of the Dawn Treader, The, 66

Waiting for Godot, 125
Walsh, Jill Paton, 75, 91, 93, 111, 149
Walters, Hugh, 114
War of the Worlds, The, 168
Warrior Scarlet, 98, 99
Watkins-Pitchford, D J, 14, 133
Watts, Stanley, 149
Wayne, Jennifer, 75
We Couldn't Leave Dinah, 28
We Didn't Mean to go to Sea, 83–84
Weathermonger, The, 100, 120
'Weaving of Fairy Tales, The', 51
Webb, Kaye, 38
Weber, Alfons, 71
Weir, Rosemary, 111
Weirdstone of Brisingamen, The, 113
Welch, Ronald, 32, 111, 112
Wells, H G, 168
Wezel, Peter, 53
When Marnie was There, 102
Where/On Parents and Law, 177

Where the Wild Things Are, 38, 43–46, 58
Whispering Mountain, The, 108
White, T H, 120, 131
Whitlock, Pamela, 91
Widdershins Crescent, 33
Wildsmith, Brian, 48, 53, 54
Willard, Barbara, 73, 93, 112
Williams, Ursula, Moray 70
Williams-Ellis, Amabel, 130, 132
Wind in the Willows, The, 40, 117, 122
'Windrush' books, 178
Winnie-the-Pooh, 40
Wizard of Earthsea, A, 144
Wolves of Willoughby Chase, The, 105–107
Woodford, Peggy, 149
Woolpack, The, 95
'Worrals', 18
'Worzel Gummidge Books', 72
Wright, Billy, 32
Writing on the Hearth, The, 95
Wuthering Heights, 117, 122
Wyndham, John, 100, 114
Wyss, J R, 133

Yeats, W B, 102
Yeoman, John, 56

'Zebra Books', 38
Zindel, Paul, 149